If [*Hutzler's*] doesn't become the hottest local holiday gift this year, I'll be very surpised. It's beautifully written, obviously by someone who has an affinity for department stores.
—Frederick N. Rasmussen, *Baltimore Sun*

To hear Mr. Lisicky talk, writing this book was simply his destiny.
—Alan Feiler, *Baltimore Jewish Times*

Lisicky spins the tale of the 132 year old store whose downtown store and spawns in Towson offered fashion and style before closing one by one, until all that was left was a memory.
—*City Paper* (Baltimore)

If you're interested in department store history, buy his books.
—David Sullivan, *Philadelphia Inquirer*

The position of Official Historian of East Coast Department Stores is no longer available, now that author Michael J. Lisicky has followed up *Hutzler's: Where Baltimore Shops* with *Wanamaker's: Meet Me at the Eagle*.
—Patrick Rapa, *Philadelphia City Paper*

[*Wanamaker's* is] a loving history of the store that once "defined Center City Philadelphia."
—Elizabeth Wellington, *Philadelphia Inquirer*

Wanamaker's is a wonderfully affectionate look at the Market St. store whose name, for generations, was symbolic of Philly.
—Ronnie Polaneczky, *Philadelphia Daily News*

The time is ripe for a book about Gimbels. Lisicky has built a national reputation as a department store expert, regularly answering questions online and as a radio talk-show guest.
—Elizabeth Wellington, *Philadelphia Inquirer*

[*Gimbels*] is a passionate history of an iconic store.
—Jim Higgins, *Milwaukee Journal Sentinel*

Lisicky recalls the glory days of Gimbels. It is an evocative book filled with photos and recipes.
—Marylynn Pitz, *Pittsburgh Post-Gazette*

Lisicky opens the door to a legendary department store.
—Jill Radsken, *Boston Herald*

[Retail] fans can now take a stroll down memory lane with Lisicky, a department store historian.
—Jan Gardner, *Boston Globe*

BALTIMORE'S BYGONE DEPARTMENT STORES

MANY HAPPY RETURNS

MICHAEL J. LISICKY

Foreword by Rebecca A. Hoffberger

THE
History
PRESS

Published by The History Press
Charleston, SC 29403
www.historypress.net

First published 2012
Second printing 2012

Manufactured in the United States

ISBN 978.1.60949.667.8

Library of Congress CIP data applied for.

To Danny and Sue Sachs and George Hutzler Bernstein.

Contents

Foreword

For beautiful and good mothers everywhere.

To explain the wild success of Michael Lisicky's first book on Baltimore's Hutzler's department store and its national approximates, one need only read educator and author Richard Louv's bestselling *Last Child in the Woods*. Both Lisicky and Louv bring to the minds of us Boomers our most powerfully happy, suspended-in-time, childhood moments. For Louv, it was all about the great and joyful quiet learning accomplished by our time spent building forts in the woods, playing in streams, climbing trees or just out and about in the summer night air gleefully catching lightning bugs with our friends. The gift of the "woods child" experience has now been grievously eclipsed by media-hyped fear of strangers, litigious concerns about trespassing and disrupting property in any way and the mega loss to today's children of unsupervised alone time away from adults.

Author, musician and storyteller Michael Lisicky's passion for emporiums like Hutzler's, which he experienced as the youngest of three brothers born to a mother who knew and savored her department stores like Robert Parker knows his fine wines, has been palpably focused to recall his happiest mom/kid adventure, inherent in a ride away from home—en route in his mom's station wagon to a destiny whose sheer expectation had already put a big smile inside the great Mother's heart.

Here were our mothers, not seeking the exclusive friendship of going shopping with an adult girlfriend, but who actually wanted *us* in on the fun. They really liked getting us all nicely dressed, sharing the promise of a delicious meal; and we, we loved the hum of our mothers as they played enthused docent to us—inclusive of toy departments and something called the Notions Department—to these warmly run, welcoming and supremely personal establishments. The Hutzler charge card, the only one my mother had (it looked like a metal dog tag), was our pass to extra belonging.

Let me say this: I loved Michael's first Hutzler's book that I devoured cover to cover. Yet a few details of what I loved most, that which was imprinted on my heart, were missing! Where were the figurative children's menu desserts? The upside-down cone-headed ice cream clown and, in the fall, the ice cream Judy Witch special, with its inserted hooked cookie witch nose, raisin eyes, maraschino cherry mouth and lace paper doily witch hat brim, secured at the base of the sugar cone hat (that could be dropped to be the clown collar for the clown version of the same ice cream decorated dessert)? This place played with food, and our moms and us kids both just loved it! The Hutzler's bakery, just to the right of the Towson restaurant entry, with its pink cardboard goodie boxes, was where my mom first introduced me to red velvet cake and my favorite, pink strawberry and minced cherry icing cupcakes. From there, we took sticky buns home to Dad to soften the blow of any charges!

My beautiful mother, Peggy Jane, was far from a privileged housewife. She worked hard, strung our laundry on clothesline (another bygone, fresh-smell clothes treat) and did all the household cooking and cleaning. Stuck without her own car out in the Greenspring Valley suburbia, we all savored these Dad-driven drop-offs until she learned to drive in her early forties. This is the same mom who taught me yoga that she herself only learned from a book, and who introduced me to another great escape, the love of reading, and laughter. So the monthly trip, by her side, with her one beige cashmere coat, was Mom at her much-deserved, indulged best. Both Michael and I can't believe how special going out with our mothers made us feel, as the times spent together at such shopping pavilions were our moms' personal peak experiences of civility and carefree fun. I remember the fashion shows in the Towson lunchroom, with clothes modeled by live models (one of whom was Aunt Emily, Congressman Dutch Ruppersberger's magnificent grandmother, and another a more severe-looking model with cropped black hair with a memorable stripe up the middle like a skunk!). I loved the mural of an old-fashioned Victorian country fair, painted in soft yellows, pinks and greens, along the back counter wall of the Towson Hutzler's counter, which we sat at only when the dining room was completely full. We loved eating the Hutzler's cup of crab vegetable soup and the warm little dinner rolls. I especially loved—again a figurative food—their Raggedy Ann Salad with its shaved carrot red hair.

Today, as a museum founder and director, I am struck by the ever-respectful warm welcome by handsome Towson Hutzler's general manager Mr. George Bernstein and all the excruciating attention to beautiful and fun detail at every turn, which infected me in the most delicious way and surely informed me of lessons I have put into practice at our American Visionary Art Museum. I also remember the exotic, built-in fish tank near the boys' clothing department that my mother explained helped keep the boys calm and "well-behaved." In the girls' department, I saw the obvious thyroid disorder of a super skinny, Marty Feldman–esque (due to her enormous bulging eyes) saleswoman. At first, I was scared to death of her, but she was so nice that fear quickly went away. I saw my first albino young man out with his beautiful African American mother there too, and I thought they looked so wonderfully happy being out as we were. My sister Phyllis and I saved and saved and bought a gilded sunburst mantel clock for my parents, which we could only afford because it was missing a ray and discounted to fourteen dollars. But our parents kept that broken clock in a place of honor for many years hence.

My now ninety-nine-year-old, sharp-as-a-tack father remembers Hutzler's had "the best" coffee. I got an *Eloise in Paris* book and the Eloise doll and the Poor Pitiful Pearl doll at Hutzler's. Later, when at sixteen I moved to Paris to become mime Marcel Marcau's first American apprentice, I kept a pet turtle in the bidet, just like Eloise!

Before leaving for Paris, where I would visit Galeries Lafayette when missing my mom and Hutzler's, I sort of graduated the Towson Hutzler's to going downtown with my best friend, Shira, all by ourselves. We purchased Beatles posters from Sherman's on Park Avenue and the latest records from the Beatles, Herman's Hermits, The Dave Clark Five, The Turtles, Bob Dylan, Joan Baez and especially Motown records—Diana Ross, Little Richard, Smokey Robinson and The Miracles—only at the Hutzler's Annex Record Department. They always got the newest albums before anyone else. We would then have a delicious meal at their counter restaurant. I remember seeing for the first time a young adult with Down syndrome, lovingly mentored by the expert older waitresses there.

Shira and I always had a total ball together, and we routinely took the Slade Avenue bus to the downtown Hutzler's. But the Towson Hutzler's is where, now that my mom is achingly gone, I remain, far younger, holding my mother's sweet hand, seeing her radiate such well-deserved enjoyment in this idyllic oasis of my own brief time on earth and within such elegant and wholly consciously crafted space. If there was a *Twilight Zone* episode with a suspended visit to that era of Hutzler's, I'd watch its endless reruns! The care and imagination that went into store display props rivaled Broadway sets. At Hampden Junque, I was lucky to score a Hutzler's three-foot-tall wooden, painted and clothed Alice in Wonderland. The very first Old English Sheepdog I ever saw was not live, but you would have thought so—again another exquisite Hutzler's display creation.

My late friend, the imp-like, twinkly eyed "Glorious Founder" of Kinetic Sculpture Racing, Hobart Brown, preached one great and wise truth, especially perfect for our present, responsibility-laden, harried time. Hobart taught, "Adults are obligated to have fun so that children will wish to grow older." I only wish that Hutzler's had still been Hutzler's by the time my now-adult daughters, Belina and Athena, were kids. They would have loved it.

****

Monsieur Lisicky, thank you for your gift to me to savor this moment in our parallel personal histories that was not war or sickness but abundant good soul comfort. In doing so, I join with you to honor and remember my mom, your mom and all those other great moms and their now-grown children. Hopefully we can extract and use lessons from our fond memories of those times to uplift our spirits and infuse our current actions with some of the class and joy learned during that special era. The only man I ever saw bring blush to my mother's cheeks besides my father (whom she adored) was Towson Hutzler's general manager, Mr. Bernstein. I think she was not alone. He represented nigh heavenly grace in an earthbound kind of way. May his children reading this know that he exuded dignity, charm, propriety and respect to all. With great delight in sharing with you, dear Michael, in this conspiracy of helping to capture and broadcast beautiful memories, I conclude with Confucius's wise counsel, "Forget injury, remember kindness."

—Rebecca A. Hoffberger
Founder and director of the American Visionary Art Museum

Acknowledgements

I would like to thank the following people who helped me "make one more return" to Baltimore's great department stores: Rebecca A. Hoffberger, a real visionary who truly understands how a trip downtown, or to Towson, meant a whole lot more than just shopping, I can't thank you enough; Jacques Kelly, whose memories and archives make me, and my readers, feel very lucky; Gil Sandler, a true Baltimore institution; Danny and Sue Sachs, who brought me into the extended Hutzler family; and George Hutzler Bernstein, who shakes his head every time I insist on using his middle name.

Deep appreciation goes to Doug McElrath and the staff at the University of Maryland–College Park's Maryland Room for access to their wonderfully preserved *Baltimore News American* photographic archives. A huge thank-you goes to Jay Smith, John M. Condon and the Hearst Corporation for their cooperation and generosity in allowing me to reprint many rare photos from the former *News American*; Deb Weiner, Rachel Kassman and the staff at the Jewish Museum of Maryland; Jason Domasky, Richard Parsons and the Baltimore County Public Library Legacy Web; the Baltimore County Historical Society; the staff at the Maryland Historical Society; and the staff at the Enoch Pratt Free Library's Maryland Department.

This book would not have been made possible without the assistance of the following people: Bob Eney, Dick Wyman, Liz Moser, Sandi Gerstung, Joe Nattans, Arthur Gutman, Henry Gutman, Bobbie Gutman, Don Alexander, Edwina Smith, Susan Nehmsmann, Leonard Levey, James Doran, Louise White, Peter Rosenwald, Pat Leibowitz, Bill O'Brien, David

Ettlin, Carl Horn, Alan Katz, Ann Amernick, Sandy Schmidt, Hannah Mazo, Patsy Perlman, David Hutzler, Amy Bernstein, Michael Mankovich and all the citizens of Baltimore who hunted me down and had to tell me their wonderful, funny, nostalgic, bittersweet and personal stories. Special gratitude goes to Shirley Brewer, one of Tinsel & Beau's many voices, and to the anonymous young worker at the Towson Trader Joe's who whispered into my ear during a book signing, "I know where the reindeer Tinsel & Beau are."

As always, this book would not have been made possible without the help and patience of the following people: author Jan Whitaker, who taught me that it is okay to be infatuated by department stores; my wife, Sandy, who knows how to "nip in the bud" any embarrassingly long prepositional phrase and who also feels that it's okay to be infatuated by department stores; and my daughter, Jordan, who will probably never understand why I am infatuated by department stores but goes along for the ride anyway.

Introduction

On Saturday mornings in those days, all roads, and all the streetcars rumbling along them, led to Howard and Lexington! That was where Baltimore's department store world flourished: outside, a heady concentrate of hurrying people and lingering aromas, shopping bag vendors and sidewalk hawkers; inside the stores, the stuff of dreams—to look at and to touch and admire, and sometimes even to buy! A Saturday morning trip to downtown was for so many like a trip to Oz.
—Gilbert Sandler, author and historian, April 19, 2012

I'll never forget meeting former Hutzler's executive Danny Sachs back in 2009. I had sent a message to Danny and his wife, Sue, a former buyer from Hutzler's, and told them I was writing a book about Hutzler's. I needed help, and luckily I found Danny and Sue. At that first meeting, Danny looked me straight in the eyes and said, "You write this book, just you wait." I'll never forget those words. I thought, "Yeah, yeah. Every city loved 'their' stores. What would make Hutzler's so different?"

I'm not from Baltimore, and I had no connection to the store. But I was always fascinated with Hutzler's, just as I was always fascinated by all department stores of the 1970s. I don't really know why, but I assumed that they'd always be there. I knew they were chock-full of the history and identity of their respective cities. My family made occasional trips to Baltimore, and we always stopped at Hutzler's during these trips. We sometimes stopped at other stores, especially the Stewart's on York Road, but Hutzler's was our destination. I was intrigued by Hutzler's. Was it the name, the buildings, the logo? Now, almost twenty years after the store closed, I was afforded an incredible opportunity to write about this Baltimore institution.

To be quite honest, I (naïvely) wondered, "Does anybody even remember Hutzler's? Does anybody even care about Hutzler's?" I had a reason to feel that way. I grew up near Philadelphia, and Strawbridge & Clothier was our family's store. In many ways, Hutzler's and Strawbridge's were similar. They both were solidly middle-class stores, they shared the same buying company and members of their founding families still controlled them—a real rarity in 1980s retailing. In 2006, Strawbridge's health was failing at the same time my mother's health was failing. When Strawbridge's iconic flagship store on Philadelphia's Market Street began its closeout sale, I refused to go. Strawbridge & Clothier reminded me of my mother, and I wasn't eager to say goodbye to either one. Months after the Center City store closed, I did load the family into the car on September 8, 2006. We traveled from our home in Baltimore to the Strawbridge & Clothier store at the historic Suburban Square Shopping Center in Ardmore, Pennsylvania, on its final day of operation as a Strawbridge's. The following day, the seventy-five-year-old branch store was being christened as yet another Macy's. I was ready to say goodbye to Strawbridge & Clothier, and I was comfortable doing so at its Ardmore location. I wanted to see generations of customers reminiscing. I wanted to see reporters and cameras documenting the historical event. It was the end of a Philadelphia tradition. But nobody came—nothing. It was just another day in the daily life of a business. I drove back to Baltimore thinking, "Nobody remembers, nobody cares…"

So when Danny said, "You write this book, just you wait," I practically rolled my eyes. I didn't even want to write a book about Hutzler's. I just wanted to buy one. I spent the next three months putting together the story of Hutzler's, finding employees, personalities and photographs. When I saw the first actual hard copy of *Hutzler's: Where Baltimore Shops*, I was thrilled. But I still had that memory of my Strawbridge's visit in my head, and I wasn't sure that anybody would buy the book. "You write this book, just you wait." Danny was right—wonderfully right. The book sold out within three days and went through five more printings to meet the holiday demand. At one of my first signings, hundreds of people waited in line for up to two hours just to get an autographed copy.

I believe the success of the Hutzler's book was due to the love and fondness that people still have for this "Maryland institution." Every person I met at these signings had a story to tell. Some of the stories were funny, some were personal and others were bittersweet. Readers tracked me down by phone, e-mail and letter. People opened their hearts and let me into their memories. It was the most amazing experience.

The other department stores were also a big part of Baltimore's culture. Danny and I joked and wondered what type of response a book about Stewart's would bring. We both had to eat our words since Stewart's was the most requested store for a second book. Then people started talking about the penguins at Hochschild's, the Washington's Birthday bargains at Brager-Gutman's and the sales and show windows at the Hecht Co. Others requested more information on the high-fashion women's store Schleisner's. These memories need to be preserved, and that's what this book is all about.

With priceless information and insights, Danny and Sue taught me about Hutzler's, but nobody taught me more about the Hutzler's mystique than a woman named Marjorie. She called me out of the blue and spoke to me for about two hours. She was as excited to talk as I was to listen. No other story defines Hutzler's history better than Marjorie's. She is a self-described "Hutzler-a-holic," and here is her story:

I am so Hutzler's. I can just smell being in there right now. There was such an aura and excitement. I would arrive and say to myself, "I'm here. Merchandise Central!"

My mother took me to Hutzler's when I was little, and I never left. The things that I bought there over the years were so gorgeous. "The nightgowns, the lingerie, Oh, save me!" Even after my son was born I went to Hutzler's in Towson every night. I would put my son to bed, my mother-in-law would come to the house and off I'd go. Once I found myself in the hospital for about thirty days. My husband walked into the store and a manager stopped him and asked, "Where is she? My sales figures have gone down!"

I liked the Occasion Extraordinaire, but I preferred the regular merchandise. My favorite sale was the EOM, or the End of the Month Sale. I would show up at the store with nothing more than my credit card, Kleenex and some lipstick. I'd wait for the opening bell to ring. Once it rang, I'd say, "Charge!" I would start in the basement and work my way all the way up to the sixth floor.

Looking west down a bustling Lexington Street from Liberty Street in 1954. *Special Collections, University of Maryland Libraries.*

I once had a job at Hochschild's, but Hochschild's was a step down from Hutzler's. Hecht's never had the warmth. Stewart's was cold and unfriendly. You had to put a coat on when you went in there. It was very straight-laced, very Roland Park, very Guilford. O'Neill's had a wonderful linen department. It was a good store, and they understood Hutzler's.

Later on, I stopped going downstairs at the downtown store. It looked too bad. It hurt me. When the store moved to the new Palace building, I went there a couple of times. It didn't have the warmth, class or ambiance of the old Hutzler's. I stopped going there because I just didn't want to admit it.

I kept shopping at Hutzler's until the store closed. I knew it was going to close, and I kept going back just trying to look for my last scraps of Hutzler's. You may ask, "Why did you stay with Hutzler's until the very end?" Well, I just couldn't let the store die by itself. After it closed, I had to wean myself off of shopping.

What was it about Hutzler's? The service was superb. The store was pristine. The aura, the ambiance, there was such finesse. The employees were so polite and were so interested in you. There was nothing like it. When Hutzler's closed, I thought that Nordstrom's was going to pick up the slack, but they didn't. You don't replace Hutzler's.

I need to thank Marjorie and every other person who shared their memories with me. It has been a true honor, and this book is dedicated to all of you. I guess Danny Sachs was right after all. "You write this book, just you wait."

Hutzler's

Where Baltimore Shopped

Baltimore Sun columnist Jacques Kelly says, "Hutzler's was a store that was better than it needed to be. Hutzler's raised the level." When Moses Hutzler helped his son Abram open a dry goods store in 1858, he could not have realized that this business would become one of Baltimore's most beloved institutions. M. Hutzler & Son opened for business on January 7, 1858, in a modest storefront on Howard and Clay Streets, formerly known as Wagon Alley. Hutzler assumed control of a business formerly operated by Elkan Bamberger, who offered embroideries, ribbons, millinery and fancy goods. Moses signed the business license for the new store because his son Abram was too young to file the paperwork. But the store was under Abram's control, and his father was never connected with the management of the firm. Abram's brothers Charles and Davis soon joined him in the business. The store was renamed Hutzler Bros. and grew in size and stature over the next 132 years.

Hutzler Bros. "One-Price House" was founded with reasonable principles: the patron should be given the best goods at the fairest prices, and those goods should always be represented "strictly as they are." The Hutzler brothers also felt that merchandise sold should always "be under-rated rather than over-rated, so that at no time should any customer be disappointed."[1] The store adhered to a one-price policy that helped the firm deal with "persistent bargain hunters." In 1867, Abram and Charles Hutzler developed a wholesale business on Baltimore Street near Hanover Street and left David in charge of the Howard Street retail store. The wholesale department was a successful operation, but the retail store grew rapidly. In 1887, the wholesale business was sold, and the three brothers joined forces to build Baltimore's next great "palace" store.

Joel Gutman & Co. built Baltimore's first palace department store in 1886. Located on Eutaw Street, Joel Gutman's ornate "75-foot Renaissance revival façade with its two-story plate-glass windows overshadowed many nearby storefronts."[2] The opulent store drew thousands of curious shoppers on its opening day.

On February 1, 1888, Hutzler Bros. started construction of its new retail store, taking the palace concept to a higher level. Designed by architect Edwin F. Baldwin and Josiah Pennington, Hutzler's new palace department store was slightly taller and slightly bigger than Gutman's emporium. At the store's grand opening on September 17, 1888, Hutzler's was cited as "one of the largest and best arranged buildings of its kind in the United States." The *Baltimore Sun* called the Romanesque-designed building, with its Nova Scotia buff stone and wide Moorish arch, "a credit to Baltimore and its workmen...a monument to the enterprise."[3]

The year 1888 also marked the birth of Hutzler's famous promotion, the Occasion Extraordinaire. The event's unusual name is credited to David Hutzler, although some reports show the term "occasion extraordinary" used as far back as 1883.[4] After returning from a trip to Paris, David Hutzler told his workers, "We're going to have a wonderful bargain in every department, and we're going to call the sale 'The Hutzler Occasion Extraordinaire.'" Hutzler stressed, "Baltimore women do NOT have to take a French course to know that at Hutzler's, an Occasion Extraordinaire means a bargain sale."[5] The sale was originally "an occasion when we close out, at extraordinarily low prices, all old lots and remnants that have accumulated." In the early 1900s, O'Neill's and Stewart's used the OE term during some of their promotions, but the practice didn't last. The name "Occasion Extraordinaire" clearly belonged to Hutzler's in Baltimore. During the life of the business, except during the war, Hutzler's Occasion Extraordinaire was an important tradition.

In 1908, the store celebrated its fiftieth anniversary, and the firm incorporated as Hutzler Brothers Company. The same year, the store commissioned a painting entitled *The Baltimore Girl* by artist Harrison

Fisher. Fisher was asked to draw the "real" Baltimore girl, a "truly lovely maiden," in honor of the anniversary. The painting was forever linked with Hutzler's, and critics stated, "There was no more charming creature extant than 'the Baltimore Girl.'" The celebrated painting was housed in the ninth floor's Executive Offices, not far from the famous wooden china cabinet, a gift from David Hutzler to Ella Hutzler in 1888. It was built in the shape of the 1888 palace store. Both artifacts are now in the possession of the Jewish Museum of Maryland.

Hutzler's famous Executive Training Program was inaugurated in 1921. This important program helped advance the professional lives of many Baltimoreans who were new to the workforce. Initially, the program was designed to "teach new employees the fundamentals of their job, assist all employees to do their present job better, and help them prepare for promotion."[6] Hutzler's Executive Training Program was open to college graduates and store employees who had earned the opportunity to become store executives. Interns were expected to participate in a three-month training course, which exposed them to every facet of Hutzler's business organization. Future executives learned how invoices were processed in Accounts Payable; they became skilled at customer complaint resolution in the Bureau of Adjustment; and they studied competitive pricing in the Comparison Department. The Executive Training Program also provided financial assistance to participants who enrolled in beneficial courses at Johns Hopkins University. By 1958, Hutzler's boasted, "85% of our present junior and senior executives were promoted from within the organization due to the Executive Training Program."

Even during some of the country's most difficult economic times, Hutzler's physical plant continued to grow. In 2009, the late Richard Hutzler said, "I remember the store expanding during the depths of the Depression. I remember dad [Albert Hutzler Sr.] saying, 'only the Pennsylvania Railroad and Hutzler's were damn fools to go into big expansions during the Depression.'" However, the store "made enough money" during that time, and the family suffered very little hardship. Major additions to Hutzler's were completed in 1916, 1924 and 1929. The company's most significant project was completed on October 11, 1932, when "Greater Hutzler's" added yet another building to its compilation of many different storefronts. The Art Deco structure was the building that most Baltimoreans identified with Hutzler's. The six Hutzler buildings contained over 170,000 square feet of selling space, a

The flagship Hutzler's department store on Howard Street, as seen in the 1970s. *Courtesy of the Baltimore County Public Library Legacy Web.*

Downstairs Store that operated autonomously from the main floor, three restaurants, an underground tunnel that connected the main store with the Saratoga Street Annex and a seven-story parking garage. The tunnel that ran underneath Saratoga Street was designed to keep shoppers out of inclement weather and was accessible through the Downstairs Store. Buyer Sue Gaston Sachs says, "The tunnel was about twelve feet wide and tiled, and it wasn't very fun. You had to sort of walk uphill and end at an elevator. The tunnel was kind of creepy." The parking garage not only helped find a solution to downtown's parking challenges but also offered customers conveniences such as oil changes, tires, batteries and car washing. But most people remember the garage for its sharp, tire-squealing, hairpin curves.

The strength and presence of its family members drove Hutzler's popularity and success, especially during the first half of the twentieth century. A three-person family team comprised Hutzler's leadership. Albert Hutzler Sr. was the company's longtime president, his brother Joel was the operational and financial director and cousin Louis was in charge of merchandising. Hutzler family member George Bernstein says, "Hutzler's was a real family store when Albert was there. He was very bright and very competent." Joel Hutzler was less outgoing than his brother Albert, but he still had a high-profile presence throughout the store. The *Baltimore Sun* called Joel "gentle and soft-spoken socially, but his piercing eyes gave indication of the decisiveness that characterized his actions at the boardroom table."[7] Joel's son, David A. Hutzler, expands on that characterization: "My father once told me that every business has to have a bad guy. It keeps the business on its toes." Cousin Louis was the true merchant. Louis Hutzler began working in the store as an assistant buyer in 1901 and eventually retired as the store's chairman in 1950. Buyer Bill O'Brien remembers, "Albert and Joel took turns walking up and down the floors, talking to everybody. They'd routinely ask the elevator operators about their mothers or their children." By the mid-1950s and 1960s, later generations joined the company to mixed reviews. Business disagreements led to family infighting behind the doors of the Executive Offices. But Baltimorean customers were comfortable walking the aisles, side by side, with Hutzler family executives.

The 1940s were an interesting time for the store. In 1942, a five-story extension to its Art Deco storefront created an additional forty thousand square feet of floor space. Like all Baltimore department stores, Hutzler's was active in the war bond effort. In 1943, Hutzler's

An interior view of the 1888 Hutzler's palace building in the 1950s, featuring Nofade woven cotton dresses. *Courtesy of Jacques Kelly.*

A view of Hutzler's Downstairs Store and its "Hutzler's Hikers" children's shoe department. *Courtesy of Jacques Kelly.*

The 1932 Art Deco Hutzler's building, showing Clay Street running through the Hutzler complex. *Courtesy of the Baltimore County Public Library Legacy Web.*

"Victory Window" on Howard Street sold over $2 million in war bonds. In 1944, downtown started to feel some changes. President Albert D. Hutzler spoke about "a spreading right of blight that threatened to choke the city's vital center."[8] He advocated the construction of a crosstown expressway. Residents began to leave Baltimore for the city's suburban communities, and many of Baltimore's commercial business leaders followed their customers. Hutzler's saw its fiercest competitor, Hochschild, Kohn, branch out to Edmondson Village in 1947, and Belvedere did the same in 1948.

On June 22, 1950, Hutzler's broke ground on a plot of land in suburban Towson, beginning "one of the most extensive projects of its kind on the eastern Seaboard."[9] The product of two years of planning, the new store was conceived and planned on a much larger scale than any other branch store in Baltimore. On November 24, 1952, Hutzler's "dream came true" in suburban Towson. The store provided the same complete levels of merchandise and service that the "mother store" offered on Howard Street. The opening day advertisement read:

> *The welcome mat is out! Monday's the day! Come celebrate with us. We're oh, so proud of our new baby—our big, beautiful branch store in the heart of Baltimore County.*
>
> *Designed for your shopping delight…so lovely, so spacious, so excitingly modern in conception…Hutzler's Towson is truly a store for tomorrow, the store that you've been waiting for.*

This and next two pages: A brochure and store directory celebrating the 1952 grand opening of Hutzler's Towson. *Collection of the author.*

HUTZLER BROTHERS CO.

A Maryland Institution since 1858

now brings you

HUTZLER'S TOWSON... large, beautiful

branch store in the heart of Baltimore County . . .
ideally located for the convenience of suburban and
country dwellers. Designed for your shopping delight
. . . so lovely, so spacious, so excitingly modern in con-
ception . . . Hutzler's Towson is truly a store of tomorrow, the store that you've been waiting for. You'll find:

- *large stocks of quality merchandise for the whole family*
  - *superior free parking facilities* *air conditioning*
- *typical Hutzler service and concern for your every need*

UPPER LEVEL

Here is your Home Floor . . . your Home Sewing Floor too.
Highlight...a charming restaurant, the Valley View Room
. . . where a dramatic floor-to-ceiling glass wall invites
you to enjoy the beautiful sweep of the valley to the north.

Art Needlework	Rest Rooms	Offices
Bake Shop	Toys	Patterns
Check Room	Trimmings, Buttons	Repair Desk
China and Glass	Upholstery	Restaurant—
Draperies	Will Call	Valley View Room
Fabrics		
Housewares		
Lamps		
Linen Shop		
Lounge		
Notions		

MIDDLE LEVEL

Here . . . a bright and playful atmosphere for the Young World, equipment specially sized for children. Men's and Boys' departments are smartly tailored to masculine taste. Gift seekers will delight in the uniquely designed Gift Shop.

Books
Boys' Wear
Candy
Children's Accessories
Children's Wear
Gift Shop
Girls' Wear
Infants' Shop
Luggage
Men's Clothing
Men's Furnishings

Shoes—
    Boys', Children's,
    Girls', Men's

Silverware
Stationery
Teen Shop

LOWER LEVEL

A Woman's World—all lovely color and texture and green growing plants. Enchanting place to choose an entire wardrobe . . . and so cleverly arranged for shopping comfort.

Aprons, Uniforms
Beauty Shop
Blouses
Children's Barber Shop
Coats—Better, Budget
Collegienne Shop
Corsets
Dresses—Misses', Women's,
    Casual, Budget, Maternity,
    Pin Money
Fashion Accessories
Gloves
Handkerchiefs
Hosiery
Jewelry

Leather Goods
Lingerie
Lounge
Loungewear
Millinery
Rest Rooms
Shoes

Separates, Sweaters
Suits—Better, Budget
Sun Shop
Toiletries
Valley Shop—
    for Suits, Dresses,
    Bridal Wear

Hutzler's

*You'll find large stocks of quality merchandise for the whole family,
superior free parking facilities, service in the Hutzler tradition. You'll lose
your heart to Hutzler's Towson—Maryland's newest department store.*

On opening day, the Towson store ribbon was cut simultaneously
by Joel G.D. Hutzler, Charles G. Hutzler, Albert D. Hutzler Jr., Louis
Hutzler and Henry Oppenheimer, former chairman of Hutzler's and
husband of Cora Hutzler. The executives, who had worked feverishly
to ready the store in time for the Christmas selling season, were
"poised and glowing with customer compliments." The Hutzler in-
store magazine *Tips and Taps* emotionally described the Towson store's
opening day:

> For many months Hutzler's Towson has been on our lips and in our
> hearts. On November 24 it became a reality! We announced its debut with
> pride and satisfaction—and in the hope that it would fill an important
> place in the needs of the community. Opening in full Christmas regalia,
> it presented a dramatic spectacle both inside and out...Its debut climaxed
> the 95th year of Hutzler Brothers Company, a Maryland Institution
> since 1858.[10]

George Bernstein says, "Towson was right in the middle of our
customers." His father, Marcus Bernstein, was a popular former manager
of the Towson store and was known by shoppers and employees as a
"terrific and gentle guy."

From its acres of free parking, late-night hours and well-organized
store layout, Hutzler's Towson gave its suburban customers a "pleasant,
convenient, and efficient background for shopping." It also gave its
suburban customers one less reason to go downtown.

On October 7, 1956, Hutzler's Eastpoint opened for business in
the Eastpoint Shopping Center in eastern Baltimore County. Unlike
the Towson store, Eastpoint carried only "large stocks for apparel and
accessories that catered to the fashion needs of this rapidly growing
community." Downgrading its offerings at the store, Hutzler's Eastpoint
was an "upgraded basement-store operation" that veered perceptibly
from the downtown parent's image.[11] Hutzler's was known for its quality,
upscale merchandise, and the downscaled store confused and angered the
local customer base. "We made Eastpoint a budget store and it slapped
the community in the face," says one former employee. "If Towson was

The popular Art Deco escalator bank inside Hutzler's Towson. *Courtesy of the Baltimore County Public Library Legacy Web.*

HUTZLER'S
eastpoint
Eastern Avenue and North Point Road, Baltimore 24, Maryland

A postcard of Hutzler's Eastpoint store featuring Hutzler-quality merchandise at attractive prices. *Collection of the author.*

where our customers were, Eastpoint was where we had no customers," adds Bernstein. Regardless, Hutzler's mistakenly underestimated the preferences of the industrial workers in the East Baltimore area.

In the fall of 1958, Hutzler's Westview became the company's third suburban store. The three-level store was located six miles west of downtown Baltimore at the intersection of Baltimore National Pike and the proposed Baltimore Beltway. The store was designed to be larger than the Towson Hutzler's, and the company hoped that Westview would mimic the success of Towson. Westview maintained a strong loyal clientele, but it was located in a totally unpopulated area when it was built. At the time of its opening, Hutzler's Westview was viewed by retail analysts as "the first Baltimore department store to have invaded Washington's retail territory."[12] Although Hutzler's Westview store was located thirty-two miles from the Washington boundary line, the Washington newspapers refused to allow Hutzler's to advertise in their papers out of loyalty to the local Washington retailers. Edwina Smith completed Hutzler's Executive Training Program and worked at the Westview store for two years. "Westview didn't have the high-priced merchandise. There were just certain things we didn't carry that we

Hutzler's Westview shortly before its grand opening in September 1958. *Courtesy of the Baltimore County Public Library Legacy Web.*

The downtown Hutzler's in 1958, celebrating the company's 100th anniversary. *Courtesy of Jacques Kelly.*

Albert D. Hutzler Sr. addresses a crowd of Hutzlerites in the store's Colonial Restaurant regarding the store's 100th birthday celebration. *Courtesy of Jacques Kelly.*

should have," says Smith. Nonetheless, Hutzler's Westiview helped the company create a circle around Baltimore city.

Hutzler's marked its 100th anniversary in 1958 with a yearlong schedule of special sales, unique exhibits, visiting celebrities and historical presentations. Mammoth birthday cakes and a replica of the original M. Hutzler & Son storefront at Howard and Clay Streets graced the exterior of the downtown Howard Street store. The Hutzler Centennial Exposition was held from February 24 through March 1, 1958. Special demonstrations were featured throughout the Howard Street store, especially on the fifth floor. Products such as Lenox China, General Electric appliances and Flint Cutlery were featured. Demonstrations included broom-making by the Maryland Workshop of the Blind and glass blowing by Corning. Outside the Colonial Restaurant, the Martin Company sponsored a Vanguard missile display. The store featured a special Centennial rose pattern on certain fabrics and Centennial gold wrapping paper.

Hutzler's owned the front page of the Society section of the *Baltimore Sun*'s Sunday edition, as well as a quarter-page advertisement on page three of the weekday *Sun*. Merchandise managers and buyers fought among themselves for this advertising space. "We wanted that [advertising space] more than anything," says Dan Sachs. For many years, the legendary Hazel Croner drew Hutzler's Society page advertisement. Hazel originally worked at the Hecht Company but later joined Schleisner's, Baltimore's high-end women's ready-to-wear clothing store, until she eventually moved to Hutzler's. Former employee Louise White was awestruck by Hazel Croner and feared her abilities and stature. White remembers:

> *Hazel Croner was an absolute terror. Hazel had been the art director at Schleisner's before Hutzler's got her. It was a grand coup. Hazel designed all of the front-page ads from the Society page. She could make a model sweep off the page. I was always scared to walk by Schleisner's. In May 1964, a Society page advertisement was going to feature the bikini. Hazel sent the proof off to the* Sun. *But when the proof came back, the model's belly button was removed. [Hazel] was in a frenzy. The advertising director from the* Sun *told Hazel and the Hutzler's staff, "The* Sunpapers *do not publish belly buttons."*[13]

Shortly afterward, the *Sun*'s advertising director paid Hutzler's—and Hazel—a personal visit. He presented Hazel with a small gift-wrapped box. Inside was the metal copy plate of the missing belly button. Hazel Croner worked for Hutzler's well into the 1980s and passed away on October 27, 2011, at age ninety-eight.

Hutzler's had a strong reputation for quality merchandise, both locally and nationally, throughout the 1960s. In 1962, the company debuted its in-store Valleybrook Shop, which offered high-end clothing that catered to the "growing interest in casual living." Hutzler's enjoyed its membership in the Associated Merchandising Corporation (AMC), a marketing and research organization that provided its member stores with information about buying trends, fashion direction and product development.[14] Other stores affiliated with AMC's buying services were Abraham & Straus in Brooklyn, Filene's in Boston, Joseph Horne in Pittsburgh, Burdine's in Miami, Hudson's in Detroit and many others. Membership in AMC gave Hutzler's considerable buying power. George Bernstein states, "AMC got Hutzler's into buying offices that we shouldn't have gotten into." Hutzler's buyer Sue Gaston Sachs remembers vendors

Hazel Croner's famous bikini advertisement in the May 3, 1964 *Baltimore Sun*'s Society page. The *Baltimore Sun*'s publishers refused to print the model's belly button, infuriating Croner. *Collection of the author.*

"going crazy for you" in the New York fashion market: "Hutzler's had a very good national reputation. As buyers, we could walk into a buying office in New York and the vendors would want our order so badly. We were small, but they treated us like equals. We were the prestige store of Baltimore. For the vendors, it was just an honor to get your merchandise into Hutzler's."

Stewart's also had a reputation for carrying quality merchandise, but it could never match the reputation or stature of Hutzler's. One Hutzler's

Hutzler's annually distributed approximately 250,000 calendars to its most important customers. The 1965 calendar helped celebrate the opening of Hutzler's Southdale store in Anne Arundel County. *Collection of the author.*

buyer remembered seeing a vendor leave the Stewart's store on Howard Street and walk across the street into Hutzler's. The Hutzler's buyer demanded to know why the vendor went to Stewart's before she went to Hutzler's. The vendor said, "Don't worry. They [Stewart's] bought all of the wrong colors."

On June 5, 1965, Chairman Albert D. Hutzler Sr. passed away at the family's estate, Pomona, in suburban Pikesville. The *Baltimore Sun* called Albert Hutzler Sr. "a merchant philanthropist in the Baltimore tradition of Enoch Pratt and Johns Hopkins."[15]

Hutzler's opened its fourth suburban store on October 14, 1965, at the Southdale Shopping Center in Glen Burnie. Located in a former Super Giant discount store, the one-story Southdale location was designed to serve customers in Anne Arundel County, Annapolis, southern Maryland and the Eastern Shore. "Southdale was our attempt to be all around the city," says Hutzler family member George Bernstein. Hutzler's did not open another branch store for eleven years.

In the 1970s, Hutzler's reigned supreme as Baltimore's premier department store in terms of sales and quality of merchandise. It was one of only five stores in the United States that offered Godiva chocolates.[16] Special events and festivals were held at the downtown store to encourage suburban shoppers to travel to Baltimore's inner city. Even as the store and the city faced challenges, Hutzler's Occasion Extraordinaire continued to be a phenomenal draw for customers to all Hutzler's stores. The event that originated as a winter clearance sale in 1888 became a special promotional sale held every October. The OE featured specially purchased items that were approved by a "hard boiled committee." The merchandise was usually unique to Baltimore and was sold for at least 20 percent off the suggested retail price. Many shoppers saw the two-week Occasion Extraordinaire promotion as a perfect opportunity for pre-holiday purchases.

Customers enjoyed features unique to the downtown Hutzler's, such as its signature narrow wooden escalators. George Bernstein recalls:

The escalator had these wide wooden treads. Sometime in the 1960s, women's heels were getting narrower, and their heels were getting stuck. We went to Otis and learned that it would be too expensive to replace the escalators. We had our chief engineer, Emory Perky, design and fabricate new treads and saved us a fortune. There was nothing these guys couldn't do.

Many downtown shoppers entered Hutzler's through its Saratoga Street doors, which led to Hutzler's balcony. Buyer Sue Gaston Sachs says, "Most people liked to enter Hutzler's from Saratoga Street because you got this overview. If you were sitting on the bench [on the Saratoga Street balcony], you could look out at the whole main floor. It was like sitting on the boardwalk." *Baltimore Sun* writer Jacques Kelly also feels that Hutzler's balcony helped make the store a better experience for its loyal customers. He cites the "smell of the bakery" and "the anticipation of meeting friends" as part of the Hutzler's experience that began on the balcony. "It was an easy place to drop somebody off. The balcony was a very happy place," says Kelly. The balcony was also home to the store's famous "message book." In this pre-technological era, shoppers left notes for one another in this simple spiral-bound notebook. Gil Sandler recalls, "You could always run through the messages and check out who was downtown, and where they were going to be and what they planned to do. It was a virtual message center for downtown shoppers. It was a wonderful system, reliable, indispensable."[17] "The balcony idea was pure Hutzler's, providing a depth of inventive personal service that bonded customer to institution in a way never duplicated, before or since, by any other retailer," says Sandler.

In spite of its prestigious image, Hutzler's faced serious internal struggles during the 1970s. David A. Hutzler says, "The store wasn't making money, but it was still spending like it was making money." George Bernstein recalls coming back from an AMC conference where he learned about Federated Department Stores' recent successes and promotions. He tried to convince his uncle, store president Albert Hutzler Jr., to mimic some of those programs at Hutzler's. Albert discouraged his nephew. "We do not do things like Federated," Albert told George, to which George replied, "Yeah, they make a profit and we don't!" Hutzler's did not reduce its advertising budget, but it cut corners on cleaning, maintenance and employee hours.

In July 1972, Honolulu-based retail conglomerate AMFAC (American Factors), the operators of Liberty House and Joseph Magnin department and specialty stores, announced a merger agreement with Hutzler's that involved an exchange of stock. Unable to reach a consensus on "important details," the merger between AMFAC and Hutzler's was abruptly called off one month later.[18]

In the fall of 1976, Hutzler's inaugurated a small branch store at the Salisbury Mall on the Eastern Shore. The store achieved modest success,

The main floor of the downtown Hutzler's in the early 1970s. *Courtesy of Jacques Kelly.*

and its opening was part of the company's new "grow or die" strategy. "You're not growing when you open a small store in a distant town," says George Bernstein.

Concerns were expressed about the viability of downtown Baltimore as a retail and social core. Excessive capital was needed to keep the Howard Street store maintained and competitive. "As downtown business began to deteriorate, you had this big hulking store that you didn't need anymore," says George Bernstein. Yet the iconic downtown Hutzler's hung on, inspiring admiration and loyalty among shoppers and employees. Louise White remembers the downtown store, so steeped in tradition: "There was something about seeing the downtown Hutzler's with all of its flags up. They must've had ten flags. You'd see the flags up and the awning down and off you'd go. It was a celebration. It was like a fair."

Unlike many of Baltimore's other department stores, generations of families worked at Hutzler's. Buyer Bill O'Brien says Hutzler's employees

Hutzler's small apparel-only location opened at the Salisbury Mall in 1976. *Collection of the author.*

stayed for a lifetime. "I replaced somebody who had been there for forty years. He started out as a stockboy and worked his way up," says O'Brien. Bill Ettlin, the father of former *Baltimore Sun* editor David Ettlin, worked as a hat buyer at the Howard Street Hutzler's. In the early 1950s, Bill Ettlin frequently appeared as the groom in store bridal shows because he resembled film actor Franchot Tone. George Bernstein acknowledges that the store had a staff of the most loyal employees. "You were willing to work for less if you worked for Hutzler's," says Bernstein. "Unfortunately, raises were arbitrary and nothing was objective with personnel matters."

Executive Dan Sachs says, "Hutzler's stood behind its merchandise. The store was always the leader in Baltimore, and they were very creative with everything that they did." Columnist Jacques Kelly equates "the Hutzler Guarantee as being an insurance policy." And Gil Sandler feels, "You were in a retail environment that was the most and the best. Hutzler's was the best we had." Former employee Louise White saw Hutzler's as an establishment that afforded everything to its customers. "I always felt that if the bottom dropped out, you could live at Hutzler's," says White. "You could be locked in and become some sort of *Phantom of the Opera* character and still survive."

Better Try Hochschild, Kohn

When you buy, better try Hochschild, Kohn,
It's the store Baltimore calls it own,
You'll find everything that's good there,
Your needs are understood there,
At Baltimore's own Hochschild, Kohn.
—*WBAL radio jingle, written by Rosa Rosenthal Kohn*

If any department store in Baltimore gave Hutzler's a run for its money, it was Hochschild's. Hochschild's did not have the prestige that surrounded Hutzler's, but it was a popular store, located exactly at the corner of Howard and Lexington Streets. Family executive Dick Wyman says, "There was a tremendous interchange between Hutzler's and Hochschild's, and most people had charge accounts at both stores." With a very strong line of basic merchandise, Hochschild's was seen as "the people's store." Columnist Jacques Kelly states, "Hochschild's sold what you needed, not what you aspired to get." However, Hochschild's was not perceived as a low-end store, and the two stores were fierce competitors.

Max Hochschild was only twenty-one years old when he opened his first store in 1877. "It was a real hole in the wall," said Hochschild. "I had one saleswoman and I did everything, including washing the window."[19] Like most early dry goods stores, Hochschild sold lace, ribbons and notions. His small ten-foot-wide storefront, located on

Gay Street in the city's Old Town section, soon outgrew its quarters. In 1883, Hochschild built a new three-story structure just two doors away from his original store. The newly named Hochschild's One-Price House was an elegant establishment that contained the first passenger elevator on Gay Street.

Louis and Benno Kohn were two of Hochschild's friends. They operated a clothing store on South Charles Street that was founded by Bernhard Kohn in 1862. Both Hochschild and the Kohn brothers wished to relocate and expand their businesses, and both parties picked the same location at the same time. Hochschild and the Kohns pooled their resources, formed a partnership and built Baltimore's newest department store palace at the intersection of Howard and Lexington Streets. Construction of the five-story building, designed by architect Joseph Evans Sperry, began in May 1897. Its distinctive exterior included three-story arched windows with terra-cotta balconies and polished Georgia marble panels, while its interior contained bronzed iron electric elevators and "handsomely appointed waiting and toilet rooms for ladies."[20] On November 15, 1897, Hochschild, Kohn & Co. officially commenced business and advertised "just a little more quality, just a little less price."

Although Hochschild, Kohn & Co. opened with 18,000 square feet of selling space, the company immediately added more stories and acquired more buildings to keep up with customer demand. By 1912, the store had expanded seven times and, at over 207,000 square feet, was eleven times larger than originally planned. The *Baltimore Sun* praised the business and said, "The growth of the establishment reads like the life story of a merchant prince, and such, in fact, it is, only there is more than one prince."[21]

Throughout the country, many retail families were important figures in the cultural and social lives of their respective cities, and Baltimore was no different. Prominent Jewish families founded most of Baltimore's large retail stores, and many of these family members were close with one another. Max Hochschild referred to his marriage to Lina Hamburger as his "most important venture." Isaac Hamburger, Lina's father, opened a small men's clothing store on Harrison Street in January 1850 and built a thriving one-price business with the promise of "Your Money Back On Demand." On April 5, 1911, Max and Lina's daughter, Gretchen, married Albert D. Hutzler at the Hotel Belvedere.

The partnership between Max Hochschild and the Kohn family members was a profitable one. Hochschild, Kohn & Co.'s business was

Hochschild, Kohn anchored the intersection of Howard and Lexington Streets. This scene from 1948 promotes the store's fifty-first anniversary. *Special Collections, University of Maryland Libraries.*

based on certain principles: "an acute awareness of the importance of the individual customer, fair prices, complete stocks, a one-price policy, a well-trained sales staff, honesty in advertising, a generous credit policy, and guaranteed satisfaction with every purchase."[22] From day one, the store's written policy was "Reliable goods only, at uniformly right prices. For all articles returned, if uninjured, and within a reasonable time, we shall willingly refund money." By the end of World War I, the store's annual sales volume was almost $11 million. In later years, the family reflected, "[Hochschild, Kohn] was not known as a high fashion store; its volume was in the middle to better price range, and for its volume, it depended on its interesting and aggressive promotion, its broad stocks, its competitive pricing—but most of all, on its goodwill."

Family executive Dick Wyman recalls the old Hochschild, Kohn store at Howard and Lexington Streets as a "compilation of many different buildings that was poorly configured." Even with all its expansions, the store always seemed a little too small for the amount of business realized, especially during downtown's heyday in the first half of the twentieth century. In the early 1920s, the store was overcrowded with merchandise, and the company feared that its business would suffer as shoppers switched to competitors with plentiful space. On December 10, 1923, Hochschild, Kohn & Co. announced its intention to purchase a city block bounded by Howard, Franklin, Park and Center Streets. Hochschild, Kohn planned to build a new $4 million department store just north of the immediate Howard and Lexington shopping district. The plan's supporters acknowledged that the store's relocation would not only make an ample, modern retail structure available to Hochschild, Kohn but would also help spread the congested retail shopping district northward. Max Hochschild stated, "We are going to give Baltimore a store which will be worthy of our city."[23] He promised an intensive study of America's most modern department stores and admitted that it would be several years, at least, before construction would begin.

Max Hochschild grew impatient with the company's hesitation to move forward with the store's relocation. As the price tag for a new building kept growing, Benno and Louis Kohn could not decide whether or not to assume such a financial risk. In 1926, Hochschild told his business partners, "Either we go ahead at all possible speed, or I sell out and retire." The ultimatum did not convince the company to leave its structure at Howard and Lexington Streets. In June 1927, Max Hochschild sold his stake in the firm to members of the Kohn family and announced his retirement from the presidency of Hochschild, Kohn & Co. The *Baltimore Sun* reported:

> *Having decided to enjoy the fruits of fifty-seven years of arduous work during which he and his two partners, Benno Kohn and Louis B. Kohn, have built one of the largest merchandising businesses in Baltimore and the South, Max Hochschild, president of Hochschild, Kohn & Co., has announced to his board of directors that he will retire from active business this summer…He insisted that the success of his business could not be attributed to himself alone. Would he be bored with nothing to do? Not as long, he concluded, as he can return to the store, to greet his friends and employees, and know that he is always welcome.*[24]

Better Try Hochschild, Kohn

The main floor of the downtown Hochschild, Kohn store showing crowds during the 1962 holiday season. *Special Collections, University of Maryland Libraries.*

For the next three decades, Max Hochschild maintained an office at the store where he would "just sit around and loaf."[25] Hochschild visited the store every day and helped counsel the store's management. He made several appearances at public and private celebrations, especially at the company's famous Founder's Day Dinners. Kohn family executive Dick Wyman recalls Max Hochschild as a short man with a very thick Germanic accent: "Whenever he addressed the employees at the anniversary dinners, Hochschild stood on a chair." Wyman remembers one specific interaction with Max Hochschild: "Once when I was a buyer, I saw Max coming across the third floor. I went up to him to say hello, and he said, 'Why are you saying hello to me? You should be greeting the customers, not me!'" Hochschild passed away on June 1, 1957, at the age of 101. Up until his final two years, Hochschild came to the store every day and diligently served his "courtesy" position.

Founding partner Benno Kohn passed away in 1929 just as the Depression was gripping the country. Hochschild, Kohn suffered severe losses during the early 1930s. In 1934, sales at Hochschild, Kohn dropped to half their volume from a few years earlier. Store improvements were put on hold until sales began to grow back. By 1937, the store and its management were back on track, and the Allied Stores Corporation made an offer to purchase Hochschild, Kohn & Co. This offer was declined, but Allied persisted with another offer in 1942. The management of Hochschild, Kohn remained uninterested in selling the business. More importantly, in 1942, Hochschild, Kohn & Co. opened its seven-story service building at Park Avenue and Centre Street. This building also housed the company's new retail furniture department and the headquarters of the home delivery service, Delivery of Baltimore. Delivery of Baltimore, Inc. was a joint cost-saving service that delivered purchases made at Hochschild, Kohn & Co., Hutzler's, Stewart's and, in later years, Hess Shoes. Almost 120 delivery trucks traveled Baltimore's streets delivering packages as small as a thimble and as large as a sofa. Before Delivery of Baltimore was established, department stores offered the option of "charge and send." Free next-day delivery service, no matter how small the purchase, was a department store amenity until rising costs, increased distance between store and customer and the advent of credit card services made such service obsolete.[26] Delivery of Baltimore, and its popular green trucks, continued until January 1983, when downtown business declined, suburban shopping centers flourished and customers found it quicker and easier to take purchases home in their cars.

Prior to World War II, the store had lost prestige and momentum, as business differences within the family affected the quality of its management and its long-term operations. By 1945, Hochschild, Kohn was back on the road to profitability. Its new family leadership team consisted of president Martin B. Kohn, vice-president/treasurer Louis B. Kohn II and vice-president/secretary Walter Sondheim Jr. Another important force in the business was Martin's wife, Rosa Rosenthal Kohn. Rosa, a former Sunday magazine writer for the *New York Times*, joined the store as its training director and became actively involved in publicity and advertising. With a flair for poetry and prose, Rosa wrote the store's famous jingle "When you buy, better try Hochschild, Kohn...," advertising themes, Founder's Day program skits and frequent articles for the monthly in-store magazine, *The Oriole*. She was a tremendously popular figure within the store and

Hochschild's popular warehouse and furniture store on Park Avenue, as seen in 1971. *Special Collections, University of Maryland Libraries.*

the community, and the family attributed much of its success to Rosa's personality and involvement.[27]

Hochschild, Kohn was a city and country pioneer in the development of branch stores. Joel Gutman & Co. developed the city's first branch store in the summer of 1928 with a small storefront at the Hotel Chateau at Charles Street and North Avenue.[28] The venture was short-lived, as the firm of Joel Gutman & Co. was liquidated the following June. However, Hochschild, Kohn had grander plans than Gutman. On June 3, 1947, Hochschild, Kohn opened the city's first branch department store at the Edmondson Village Shopping Center in West Baltimore. The Edmondson asked shoppers "to come see Maryland's first realization of the newest trend in department store retailing." President Martin Kohn stated, "Hochschild Kohn–Edmondson is but another evidence of our faith in the economic future of this city. We sincerely hope this and succeeding branch stores of our firm will reduce shopping problems by offering departmentalized services close to your homes." Visual merchandising manager Bob Eney liked the Edmondson store: "It was unique in Baltimore because it was brand-new and had a lot of style." Edmondson's opening was followed by another branch store project at the corner of York Road and Belvedere Avenue. Plans for the Belvedere store were announced in 1945, but war restrictions prevented Hochschild, Kohn from completing the structure at that time. "Belvedere was intended to be the first branch store, and its steel frame remained untouched for a number of years [due to a shortage of supplies]," says Liz Kohn Moser.[29] Max Hochschild finally cut the ribbon on the new Belvedere branch on September 28, 1948. The two branch stores were quite different from each other. "The Edmondson store was

Hochschild, Kohn & Co. opened Baltimore's first large branch store on June 3, 1947, at the Edmondson Village Shopping Center in West Baltimore. *Courtesy of the Baltimore County Public Library Legacy Web.*

The Belvedere Hochschild, Kohn store as seen in June 1949. The store most recently served as a location for Daedalus Books. *Special Collections, University of Maryland Libraries.*

in a new section of town, which was the site of many of the early racial changes," says Moser. "The merchandise and the neighborhood [at Edmondson] were not quite as good as at Belevedere." Executive Dick Wyman adds, "Belvedere was an instant success because the population around that store was an upscale population." However, the two branch stores did share one common bond: they were too small in size. Neither store carried the complete selection of the downtown Hochschild, Kohn. And the size problems of Hochschild's branches were never more evident than when Hutzler's massive suburban store in Towson opened in November 1952.

Hochschild, Kohn felt that its future was in Baltimore's growing suburban communities. By the 1950s, the company openly complained that its downtown building was "old and expansion was continually necessary."[30] In 1951, Hochschild, Kohn began aggressive development

The Eastpoint Hochschild, Kohn store's North Point Boulevard entrance as seen through the windows of a vintage car. *Special Collections, University of Maryland Libraries.*

An architect's rendering of Hochschild's Harundale store, including its new Budget Shop, from October 1963. *Collection of the author.*

at its Edmondson branch. A two-story addition was erected behind the store, expanding the building's sales space by 50 percent. Hochschild, Kohn opened its largest complete branch store, offering all merchandise departments, on October 10, 1956, at the Eastpoint Shopping Center, located at the intersection of Eastern Avenue and North Point Boulevard. The two-story, 100,000-square-foot store contained everything from a complete home and furniture department to "live penguins in a special mall-level window to delight the youngsters." On October 1, 1958, Hochschild, Kohn opened its fourth branch at the new Harundale Mall in Anne Arundel County. Designed by architectural firm Rogers, Taliaferro & Lamb, Harundale Mall was the first enclosed shopping mall on the East Coast. Hochschild, Kohn was the major anchor tenant at the $10 million shopping center. Developed by James W. Rouse, Harundale Mall's controlled temperature "permitted the growing of tropical plants, such as orchids, date palms, and lilies." Upon its opening, Harundale was the only enclosed mall in the country other than Southdale in Minneapolis. The mall was designed "to give shoppers a feeling of being out of doors—to provide psychological and visual contrast and relief from indoor shops."[31] Executive Dick Wyman says, "Harundale had a great opening. It was a beautiful store, and it did very well. Rouse always had taste." Stewart's buyer Don Alexander feels that Stewart's did not locate in Anne Arundel County because the Hochschild, Kohn store at Harundale Mall was too popular. "That [Harundale] Hochschild, Kohn store did very well from the get-go," says Alexander.

Pat Leibowitz worked for Hutzler's and Hochschild, Kohn and feels that Hochschild, Kohn was a warmer store than Hutzler's. "Hochschild, Kohn was a wonderful place to work," says Leibowitz. "[It] was a hardworking kind of store." Hochschild's met Hutzler's head-on with its special Bargain Fridays sale events, Hochschild's answer to Hutzler's Occasion Extraordinaire. The sale featured "wanted seasonal merchandise, at least 15% off, and was picked with 'love and affection' first." Friday was traditionally the slowest shopping day of the week, and Bargain Fridays gave the company a much-needed boost in sales.

Martin Kohn was the true merchandiser of Hochschild, Kohn. He walked through its aisles every day and knew everybody's names. His brother Louis was the financial expert. But if there was a "soul" at the store, it was Walter Sondheim Jr. Walter's father was Max Hochschild's uncle, who was active in the early part of the business. Advertising employee Louise White recalls Walter Sondheim as "a big, lovable, compassionate bear," and Bob

Hochschild's sixty-first anniversary sale in 1958 celebrates all six of the company's locations. *Collection of the author.*

Eney says, "Walter was a great guy, absolutely super. He liked people and he treated them like individuals." In addition to his duties at Hochschild, Kohn, Sondheim was a member of the Baltimore City School Board from 1948 to 1957. Historian Gil Sandler remembers when Sondheim's work at the department store and his work with the school board urgently crossed paths. Sandler says:

> *Hochschild's has an arrangement where they would pay the teachers at 4:00 p.m. on Fridays because the teachers couldn't make it to the bank in time. One day, Hochschild's didn't have enough cash. Sondheim called the mayor and said, "We need to pay these teachers!" It was around 2:00 p.m., and the mayor said, "If you can get here right now, we'll give you the cash." So Sondheim hired a Brink's truck and rode shotgun. By the time Walter made it back to Hochschild's with the cash, he went in one door with the cash while the teachers were coming in another door with their checks.[32]*

Better Try Hochschild, Kohn

When Brager's merged with Julius Gutman Co., Hochschild's acquired the Eutaw Street structure and relocated its furniture department. Hochschild, Kohn's downtown store, as seen in May 1960, was spread throughout eight adjacent buildings. *Special Collections, University of Maryland Libraries.*

Sondheim served as the Baltimore City School Board's president in 1954 when Baltimore became the first school district south of the Mason-Dixon line to follow the Supreme Court ruling in *Brown v. the Board of Education*. Sondheim, likewise, advocated for racial integration of the Hochschild, Kohn lunch counter and tearoom. When busloads of Morgan State students arrived downtown on March 26, 1960, to seek service in the department store restaurants, only Hochschild, Kohn served the students and implemented a nondiscrimination policy in its eating facilities. Black shoppers were not welcome at Hochschild's, nor were they at Hutzler's, Stewart's, Hecht-May and the other large stores. But Walter Sondheim convinced the store's leadership that it was time to end discrimination. Although the business decision was viewed by some as a risky choice that could alienate its traditional white customer base, Dick Wyman feels that Walter, Louis and Martin Kohn took great pleasure in the store's integration policy. Letters poured into Hochschild's executive offices supporting its "stand against discrimination." Other letters expressed anger that Hochschild, Kohn was converting into "a colored store." "[After the integration of the lunch rooms], we began promoting employees so that we had a black worker at every level," says Wyman. "We were the first store to do that. Before, blacks couldn't try on clothes [in the dressing rooms], and we changed that too."

Liz Kohn Moser remembers Hochschild, Kohn for its "quality and accessibility." "Hochschild, Kohn was good stuff at reasonable prices. The salespeople were trained to be human beings of service. Our employees were friendly and personal. I think a lot of our sales were based on that principle," says Moser. Dick Wyman calls his family's former store "a Baltimore institution." Wyman continues, "Hochschild, Kohn was a place where people who worked there liked that they worked there. It had a real esprit de corps."

By the 1960s, Hochschild, Kohn was more profitable overall than Hutzler's, its nearest competitor. Hochschild's was stronger than Hutzler's in hard goods but lagged behind in ready-to-wear. "We beat out Hutzler's on toys, housewares and cosmetics," says Dick Wyman. In 1960, Hochschild's took over the former Brager department store building on Eutaw Street and converted it into its furniture store. However, the Kohns were concerned that very few future generation family members showed an interest in operating the business. Dick Wyman was the only family member who considered managing Hochschild's and pursuing a career in retail. Louis, Martin and Dick concluded that the store's future did not rest in family hands. "We decided that we were not the kind of store that could pay stockholders a lot of money," says Wyman. "We got together and agreed that the store had to be sold." Hochschild's actively sought a buyer for its stores and found Warren Buffett, a friend of one of Dick Wyman's cousins.

Hochschild, Kohn & Co. was Warren Buffett's first private investment. The thirty-six-year-old Buffett was the owner of an Omaha-based investment company that was "constantly in search of attractive investments." Buffett purchased Hochschild, Kohn in March 1966 with the following reasoning: "I [Warren Buffett] believe that Hochschild, Kohn has the leadership, the character, and the vision to keep moving steadily ahead in an expanding community, following its established standards of customer and employee relations in a city that knows what kind of a store it is."[33]

Martin Kohn's daughter, Liz Moser, recalls the events that led to the family's decision to sell the store: "I remember my father and mother having very grim conversations at the time of the sale. My father kept saying, 'This is a good thing. Is this a good thing?' It was our life." Buffett did not play an active role in the management of the store and was not a big presence in the store. "Warren was very nice and very easy to work for," says Moser. "He knew how to let people do their own thing." Hochschild's suburban expansion had almost come to a halt by the time of Buffett's purchase. The only suburban development since Harundale was its Early American Shop at the Reisterstown Road Plaza in May 1963. Hochschild's had the sole license in Baltimore to sell Ethan Allen furniture, and the Plaza store featured this line. Unfortunately, the Plaza customer base was not interested in this style. The store was later converted into the Plaza Shop, an apparel-only store.

In 1967, Hochschild, Kohn announced plans for two large-scale branch stores in the communities of Columbia, Maryland, and York, Pennsylvania. The York store was the first Baltimore-based department store to cross state lines. Buffett questioned the viability of both stores. Dick Wyman says, "When Warren bought the company, we had commitments for new stores in York and Columbia. He told us that it was not a smart move. I had thought that if you had enough sales, you would make more money. Warren felt that Hochschild's needed to reinvest its profits into its existing stores." In the long term, Buffett was right. Buffett didn't make much money from his purchase of Hochschild, Kohn, but he used the store's assets as collateral for other purchases. Under Buffett's ownership, Hochschild, Kohn had a profitable 1967. But its sales dropped significantly in 1968, and the outlook for 1969 was even worse. Warren Buffett wanted to be rid of Hochschild, Kohn and decided to seek a buyer for the stores or liquidate the company.[34]

Buffett found Supermarkets General, a holding company that owned Pathmark supermarkets, Rickel home centers and department stores that traded under the names Genung's, Howland's and Steinbach. Supermarkets General acquired Hochschild's in December 1969 and did not divulge its purchase price. Under Supermarkets General, Hochschild, Kohn adopted a "compete-or-get-trampled-on outlook." The company's York, Pennsylvania branch opened on September 27, 1968, followed by its large Columbia Mall location on August 2, 1971. Columbia was

An interior view of the Hochschild's Security Square Mall location. The store opened in time to celebrate the company's seventy-fifth birthday. *Special Collections, University of Maryland Libraries.*

Hochschild's first suburban Baltimore-area store in ten years, but it proved to be a challenging venture. Chairman Louis B. Kohn II called the Columbia store's opening "a start of a new era for Hochschild's."[35] Columbia became the primary focus for the company, but its customer was absent. "Columbia didn't have enough customers around," says Pat Leibowitz. "But we always had to put our best merchandise in Columbia." Woodward & Lothrop, Washington's traditional hometown department store, joined Hochschild, Kohn at the Columbia Mall. "Woodies came into Columbia and took off," says Stewart's Don Alexander. "They advertised like crazy in the *Washington Post*, and most people in Columbia got the *Washington Post*. So it never brought the area's loyal Washington customers into Hochschild, Kohn."

Hochschild's next big suburban store opened on September 30, 1972, at the massive Security Square Mall in northwest Baltimore. Hochschild, Kohn president Charles Franzke called the Security Square Hochchild's "the largest most exciting store ever built for contemporary retailing in the region."[36] Security Square proved to be a financial success for the company. However, it came at the expense of its nearby Edmondson Village store, the original branch department store in Baltimore. Franzke

An employee waits for customers at Hochschild's downtown store shortly before its closing in 1977. *Collection of the author.*

The intersection of Howard and Lexington Streets is crowded with shoppers during Hochschild's "Biggest Sale" in July 1977. *Collection of the author.*

blamed Edmondson's failure on "a changing of shopping habits. The reason is economics and customers are not shopping there anymore."[37] Edmondson's closure in February 1974 was a blow to the mostly black neighborhood, but Hochschild's drop in sales volumes was too significant to justify staying open.

In August 1974, Supermarkets General appointed Ward Woods president of Hochschild, Kohn & Co. Woods was determined to make visible changes at Hochschild's. Bob Eney remembers Ward Woods assembling the employees to discuss the purchase. Eney says, "Ward told us, 'We're going to make this place great and modernize. We're going to change the way Baltimore looks.' You could hear the whole first floor groan." Woods came to Baltimore from the West Coast and was determined to replace buttoned-up collars with leisure suits. Every Tuesday, executives were ordered to wear leisure suits to work to promote the new "modern" style. Tuesday soon became Leisure Suit Tuesday. "[Ward Woods] wanted us to wear open collars, but we're a blue-collar store and sell to blue-collar people," says Eney.

Woods also made difficult decisions about Hochschild's store locations, starting with its newest branch. A store too oversized for its volume, Hochschild's left the Columbia Mall in January 1975. The store had never connected to the Washington-loyal community, and its lease was immediately transferred to the Hecht Company. Hecht's presence in both Baltimore and Washington ensured a customer base. At the end of June 1975, the York, Pennsylvania store transferred its lease to the Bon-Ton stores. York was a difficult market. Customers were loyal to local stores and needed high volumes of merchandise geared toward large sizes. Woods blamed the lack of concentrated advertising for the demise of both the York and Columbia stores, but there were many other challenges that the stores continually faced.

Max Hochschild wanted to replace the downtown Hochschild, Kohn store in 1927 because it was outmoded, awkward and antiquated. In November 1976, Hochschild's announced the removal of its central offices from the downtown store and the transfer of the 250 employees to Whitehead Road near the Security Square Mall. The move aroused suspicion that the company might abandon downtown entirely. Shoppers yearning for the old days sounded an alarm. Kathryn Frank, a loyal downtown Hochschild's shopper, said she "would die without the big old department stores." Although they were gray and faded, they remained enticing. She thought of a potential closing as "the end of the world."

Frank said, "I love these stores. If I get depressed, I come in here and remember how things used to be."[38] By the middle of 1977, Kathryn Frank had to find another place to shop downtown.

Come What May

Baltimore's largest department store building was located on the southwest corner of Howard and Lexington Streets. Its doors opened on May 22, 1925, and the new facility was described as "a place of profound beauty, distinct individuality, and unusual charm."[39] The granite structure, with its marble floors, contained a first floor that had "a ceiling as high as a modern auditorium" and an eighth floor that "presented no aspect of commercialism." The eighth-floor restaurant featured a lobby reminiscent "of a luxurious hotel, with ease, comfort and charm." For thirty years, the store operated as the May Company. But before there was the May Company, there was Bernheimer-Leader.

Bernheimer-Leader Stores was the byproduct of an August 1923 merger of Bernheimer Bros. and the Leader department stores. Brothers Ferdinand and Herman Bernheimer came to Baltimore from Hartford, Connecticut, and opened their business in 1888. Their establishment concentrated on selling low- and mid-price merchandise and was one of "Baltimore's earliest bargain houses."[40] Bernheimer's was known for a large grocery department and catered to Baltimore's burgeoning immigrant population. Arthur Gutman, grandnephew of Baltimore department store pioneer Joel Gutman, recalls Bernheimer Bros. as "a cheap ass store." Gutman continues, "If somebody questioned [the freshness of] his eggs, he [Ferdinand Bernheimer] would go ahead and eat one in front of the customer."

An eastward view of Lexington Street toward Howard Street in 1908. The original Read's store is seen in the left side of the photo, along with the former Leader store at the corner of Howard and Lexington Streets. The early Bernheimer Bros. store is seen on the right-hand side. *Special Collections, University of Maryland Libraries.*

Bernheimer's, "A City in Itself," was located on Lexington Street, a half block from Howard Street. In 1908, the company opened an elaborate annex on Fayette Street behind the Lexington Street structure. The storefront, designed by renowned architect Charles Cassell, was regarded as Baltimore's final palace department store. This ornate building attempted to shed Bernheimer's of its bargain store image. But the company still yearned to be at the corner of Howard and Lexington Streets, the center of Baltimore's retail market, and the small Leader department store stood in its way.

The Leader was founded in 1904 by the firm Kohner & Company but was purchased the following year by Maurine Cahn and Leon Coblens. Like Bernheimer Bros., the Leader was a "low grade store." Both stores outgrew their facilities. The Leader needed more space, and Bernheimer's wanted the Howard and Lexington corner location. On August 1, 1923, the two businesses merged and formed Bernheimer-Leader Stores. They

A 1925 artist's rendering of the soon-to-be completed Bernheimer-Leader Stores. The building stretched from Fayette Street all the way to a new large structure located directly at the corner of Howard and Lexington Streets. Within a couple of years, the new complex was purchased by the May Company. *Collection of the author.*

immediately began building a new massive grand store. At its 1925 grand opening, Bernheimer-Leader stated, "We cease to be mere merchants, but shoulder the responsibility of public officials." Unfortunately, the company could not shoulder the financial burden created by the formation of the new structure. Within two years, Bernheimer-Leader fell into a state of collapse, but the May Company came to the rescue.

The May Company was the nation's largest department store corporation with $108 million in annual sales and locations in Cleveland, Denver, Los Angeles, St. Louis and Akron. On September 9, 1927, the May Company took immediate control of Bernheimer-Leader's land, fixtures, building and stock. White flags with the May Company name were immediately flown from the building's flagpoles, and the brass Bernheimer-Leader nameplates were quickly removed. May Company's vice-president, Nathan Dauby, stated, "We selected Baltimore because of its strategic position, its great stability and its brilliant future. We were conscious of our ability to establish a business which Baltimore would accept with enthusiasm. While Baltimore may not have heard of the May Company, the May Company has heard of Baltimore."[41]

The former leadership of Bernheimer-Leader called the May Company's entrance into Baltimore "a good thing for them, a good thing for us, and a good thing for Baltimore." May said, "The people of Baltimore may be assured of rapid progress in the development of a typical May enterprise and the enjoyment of every facility in merchandising and service of the May organization."[42]

Though it was located at the main retail intersection in the city, the May Company kept a relatively low profile in Baltimore. It did not play a prominent role in the city's Retail Merchants Association. It offered more moderately priced merchandise than Hochschild, Kohn. Kohn family member Liz Moser says, "The May Company was a half level down from us [Hochschild, Kohn]. It was a good store, but they didn't have three generations of family members living in Baltimore." Although the company stated at its opening that it would be a Baltimore store operated by Baltimore men and women, it was viewed as an outsider. That didn't stop the business from opening a large addition on its Lexington Street side in 1941.

The May Company's most newsworthy event occurred on February 25, 1947. At 6:30 p.m., several fires broke out on the store's fifth floor and rapidly became a nine-alarm blaze. It was the largest downtown fire since the Great Fire of 1904. The fire was quickly determined to be suspicious in origin. Baltimore's fire chief, Thomas Heagerty, said that the May Company fire "looked mighty peculiar, it looks like a job for the arson squad." The store's sprinkler system had been deliberately tampered with and shut off.[43] Although firemen tried to force one thousand pounds of pressure through the store's sprinkler system, not a single drop of water came out anywhere in the store. Additionally, a potentially hazardous blaze had been discovered on the store's mezzanine the previous Wednesday and had been quickly extinguished by store personnel.

As a young child, Baltimorean James Doran spent time hanging out at his neighborhood firehouse. He vividly recalls the May Company fire:

> *I was a little kid who spent time following fire engines. All of the guys knew me. I went with the firemen to the May Company blaze. They took me into the first floor of the store, and the water was so heavy as it poured down the escalator, overflowing its sides. There were trackless trolleys that ran down Howard Street, and they had to cut the wires just to get the ladders up. One of the wires dropped and hit my shoulder. The fire burned like hell and blew out of the windows of the building's fifth and sixth floors.*[44]

The fire didn't concern patrons at the nearby Ford's Theater. Nonchalant audience members waited until the first act of *The Importance of Being Earnest* had ended before evacuating the theater.[45] With the help of the fire department's Salvage Corps, the store returned to partial operations two

A May Company advertisement from 1956 promoted the store as a complete store under one roof, unlike some of its competitors that were spread throughout many different buildings. *Collection of the author.*

weeks later. Doran says, "We used to have a Salvage Corps that didn't fight fires but instead helped commercial entities and protected their merchandise. I don't know how they reopened that store so quickly!" The fire was officially declared arson and remains unsolved to this day.

In 1953, the May Company created an exciting new restaurant called the Courtyard in its downtown store. The Courtyard Restaurant was decorated with authentic storefronts from former businesses in the city's Old Town neighborhood. The *Baltimore American* newspaper stated, "The atmosphere of Aisquith Street at the turn of the century will be recreated in the delightful, large room on the eighth floor of the department store, where delicious food will be served in the Maryland tradition." The Courtyard was a popular downtown restaurant, but it could not rival the prestige of having lunch or tea in Hutzler's Colonial Restaurant.

It took more than a new restaurant to keep the May Company competitive, and by the 1950s, the store had fallen behind in Baltimore. Executives at the St. Louis headquarters knew that the Baltimore store needed a series of suburban branches, proven growth records and strong managerial talent for the division to flourish. Even the *Baltimore Sun*, in a report on the city's retail market, stated, "It takes no crystal ball to know the old May Co. store wasn't setting the world on fire in downtown Baltimore." The quote, although ironic, was also true. Unlike the other Baltimore department stores of the time, the May Company did not operate any branches in the suburbs, only a small warehouse store on Gwynns Falls Parkway. The company realized that success could only happen by merging with a proven retail leader. The acquisition of the Hecht Company fit the bill.

Hecht's

The Hub of Baltimore

No family played a more prominent role in Baltimore's retail life than the Hecht family. The Hecht family made its fortune by selling moderation to the masses while offering liberal credit terms. Its group of stores traded under a variety of names, including the Hub, Hecht's Reliable Stores and Hecht Brothers, but most Baltimoreans just remember it fondly as the Hecht Company.

Simeon Hecht arrived in Baltimore in 1844 from the small Bavarian town of Langenschwarz. He met with his Uncle Ruben and shortly thereafter began his new life peddling goods on Maryland's Lower Eastern Shore and in Virginia's Shenandoah Valley. In 1848, Simeon returned to Baltimore and opened his own business, Hecht's Red Post Store. As he settled into his role as the successful shopkeeper of his store on Orleans Street, he sent for his family in Germany to come join him. By the mid-1850s, an anti-Semitic sentiment in Germany had grown, and many Jews felt compelled to leave their homes. In 1851, Simeon's mother, Hannah, sister Eddel and two brothers, Samuel and Reuben, came to Baltimore and started their new lives. Simeon provided financial backing for many of his family members, and by 1861, more than eight separate Hecht businesses operated out of East Baltimore.

His brother Samuel managed one of those businesses. Samuel Hecht opened a secondhand furniture store in 1857 on Broadway near Fleet Street in Baltimore's Fell's Point section. Over the years, tensions grew between Simeon and other family members, especially Samuel. Simeon was outraged that his family refused to repay their debts to him. According to Simeon, Samuel Hecht was "immoral" and a "crook." Regardless, Samuel's business continued to grow until he had to seek a larger location. In 1870, Hecht opened a new store on Broadway that featured furniture and home goods. In 1879, a clothing store, Hecht's Reliable Stores, followed nearby.

At the age of fifteen, Samuel's son Moses became the general manager of Hecht's Reliable. With his father's support, Moses convinced his family to expand the business. After opening a floor-coverings store on West Lexington Street, the family opened Hecht Brothers on Baltimore and Pine Streets in 1885. Hecht Brothers became Baltimore's largest home furnishings store. In its later years, Hecht Brothers was "a store with a history of firsts," as it introduced radios, washers, dryers and "automatic refrigerators" to Baltimore. In 1926, the company rebuilt its structure at Baltimore and Pine Streets and opened a branch store at Howard and Franklin Streets. Later, Hecht Brothers expanded to Easton and Annapolis, Maryland. Thousands of Baltimoreans, attracted to the company's deferred payment plans, opened their first charge accounts at Hecht Brothers.

Encouraged by the company's success in Baltimore, Moses opened his "dream store" in Washington, D.C., at Seventh and F Streets in March 1896. The Washington store assumed the name Hecht's Greater Stores and fell under the leadership of Moses Hecht's brother Alexander. Alexander Hecht maintained an office on the store's balcony, where he overlooked the sales floor. From this vantage point, he observed his sales force and even helped on the sales floor whenever he was needed. The store was a Washington institution, combining moderately priced merchandise with store innovations such as the city's first escalators, first department store parking garage, air conditioning and aggressive postwar suburban expansion.

Moses Hecht remained in Baltimore and wanted to expand the company's offerings in the city. He was drawn to an ornate building with a large corner display window at the corner of Baltimore and Light Streets. On October 20, 1897, he opened the Hub clothing store. Company archives say, "The grand opening at Baltimore and Light Streets was resplendent with the Washington Marine Band and the presence of Mayor Alcaeus Hooper. The affair was a dramatic one, a true herald of the great things to come for the tiny establishment."[46] The Hub was located away from the city retail epicenter of Howard and Lexington Streets, but the store developed a loyal following, especially in the menswear sector. With its Hub clothing store, Hecht Brothers home furnishings store and value-oriented Hecht's Reliable Store, the Hecht Company offered the city of Baltimore a complete merchandise selection. Although it operated a thriving department store business in downtown Washington, the Hecht firm located its headquarters at the downtown Baltimore Hub store.

In 1900, Moses opened a small department store on Fourteenth Street in New York City, expanding his empire. Hecht's New York store struggled to compete with powerful stores such as Macy's and Hearn's. Determined to make his New York store successful, Moses spent five days a week in New York manning the store and weekends back home in Baltimore.[47] This schedule continued until February 1904, when the original Baltimore Hub store succumbed to the Great Fire of 1904. Moses left the New York store in his chief executive's hands and returned to Baltimore full time. The New York store never made Moses Hecht or the Hecht business nationally known, but it remained in operation for many decades.

The Hub built a large, prominent store at the northeast corner of Baltimore and Charles Streets. This location was a bit distant from the

In 1927, the Hub completed a $700,000 addition that doubled the size of its Baltimore Street store. *Special Collections, University of Maryland Libraries.*

The Hecht Bros. store at Baltimore and Pine Streets promoted a deferred payment plan for its value-conscious shoppers. This Hecht Bros. passbook dates from 1934. *Collection of the author.*

city's core department stores but was situated right in the heart of Baltimore's financial district, along with numerous menswear shops. The store constantly expanded from neighboring building to building to keep up with its growing popularity. Throughout the Depression and other hard economic times, the Hub was a first choice for many value-minded customers. As its sister Hecht Brothers store became Baltimore's largest home furnishings store, the Hub became Baltimore's largest apparel store. A leader in the menswear market, it actively competed with the powerful I. Hamburger & Son menswear store.

The Hub was certainly not the architectural palace that defined many of Baltimore's large stores; it was merely a collection of buildings that represented the company's growing business and need for expansion. *News American* columnist Jacques Kelly stated, "The store was not a great fashion house, nor did it trade on snob appeal. It didn't have the great retail location, but the place never lacked customers."[18] Former employee James Doran recalls the look and feel of the Hub:

> *The Hub was nothing* [architecturally] *spectacular. It appeared nice and was very neat in appearance. It just wasn't in the same class of Hutzler's. The story goes that Moses Hecht would go down to the basement store [or*

Economy Store] and demand that he get his 10 percent discount. It was incredible because he owned the whole damn store!

Doran agrees that the men's store was the most prominent department at the Hub. "That's where you made money. The salesmen lived on commissions," says Doran. Former Hecht executive Peter Rosenwald remembers the Hub as "nothing unique. It was just a general department store. It was a chopped-up store that was small and inefficient." By the 1930s, the Hub had added a limited line of home furnishings, while the Hecht Brothers home store at Baltimore and Pine Streets added "cheap apparel" to its offerings. The two stores began to compete for the lower to moderate customer, although each store maintained its individual buying and managerial teams. While the two Hecht operations battled for attention, the Hub always won the popularity contest. The Hub acted

In 1927, Hecht Bros. opened an additional store at Howard and Franklin Streets. The store predominantly carried home furnishings. In March 1950, a six-alarm fire broke out on its fourth floor, killing two employees. *Special Collections, University of Maryland Libraries.*

In 1952, the Hub and Hecht Bros. merged their operations to become Baltimore's Hecht Company stores. The former Hub store at Baltimore and Charles Streets, as shown in 1957, ceased operations in June 1959. *Special Collections, University of Maryland Libraries.*

as a "general department store" and featured its popular Chestnut Room restaurant. According to Hecht family member Sandi Gerstung, "The Hub carried good clothes and had a marvelous notions department." Gil Sandler remembers the Hub "seemed like a discount store. It wasn't much of a player. The Hub was located among a lot of the menswear stores [on Baltimore Street], and that seemed to be its focus."

The 1950s were a real turning point for the Hecht family business in Baltimore and beyond. The Washington division, operating as the Hecht Company, developed large, revolutionary suburban branches in Silver Spring (November 1947) and Parkington in Arlington, Virginia (November 1951). But the significant change occurred in Baltimore. On February 1, 1952, the firm combined all six businesses under the name "the Hecht Company." However, Hecht's longtime Fell's Point businesses were not part of this consolidation. The company stated, "The combined operation in Baltimore city would make the new Hecht unit the second largest retail operation in the Baltimore area." It was officially noted that the Hub and Hecht Brothers operated competitively. The new Hecht Company stores announced, "Instead of separate credit departments, service departments, and delivery fleets, one management and one set of buyers does the whole job. Putting these stores together means lower cost of doing business."[49] On February 1, 1952, the firm combined all six of its Baltimore Hub and Hecht Brothers stores under the name "the Hecht Company."

Moses Hecht, Baltimore's final merchant prince, passed away on January 6, 1954. The *Baltimore Sun* praised Moses as "a fascinating man who embodied to a remarkable degree the American success story." Officials at the Hecht Company said, "Moses founded an institution and built a retail empire plus a host of friends and admirers." The company forged ahead after Moses's death. On September 23, 1954, the Hecht Company opened its first branch location at the Northwood shopping complex in suburban Baltimore. Executive Peter Rosenwald acknowledges Northwood's early success: "Northwood was the strongest branch for many years because of its neighborhood." The contemporary store, with its Rooftop Restaurant, courted the local working-class community. It offered moderately priced merchandise in a stylish setting. Hutzler family member George Bernstein says, "The Hecht Company was a lower-end store that catered to the lower income. As they expanded and upgraded, they became the mainstream store." Hecht family member Sandi Gerstung has fond memories of the Northwood store: "Northwood was a wonderful store. It was our first country store, and it had a different atmosphere. It was very different from the downtown store. It was much more convenient, especially for my mother."

In August 1956, the Hecht Company decided to focus its operations on the Baltimore-Washington market and closed its New York store on Fourteenth Street. The Hecht Company continued its expansion in Baltimore and opened its "store of the future" in October 1956. This second branch store was located on Edmondson Avenue in West Baltimore, opposite the city's popular Edmondson Village Shopping Center. The Hecht Company Edmondson was "a complete fashion world for our fair lady" and included a popular on-site Hot Shoppes Restaurant. Edmondson never matched the success of the Northwood store, but both branches reinvented the Hecht Company's position in the Baltimore market from a hodgepodge of oddly located aging downtown facilities to modern and convenient suburban shopping destinations.

An architectural rendering of the Hecht Company Northwood store from April 1953. *Collection of the author.*

The Hecht Company opened its second Baltimore branch in October 1956, opposite the Edmondson Village Shopping Center. *Special Collections, University of Maryland Libraries.*

The Hecht Company was a profitable department store business with strong suburban branches, and the May Company was a profitable department store business that operated an updated prominent and profitable structure at Howard and Lexington Streets. Hecht coveted the city's core location, and May wanted to compete in the suburbs. In 1958, the May Company was a national powerhouse with $533 million in sales, and Hecht was a strong regional business with $105 million in annual sales. In October 1958, a merger between the two organizations was announced. It had the makings of a perfect marriage. The purchase gave May a prominent regional East Coast presence. At the time, Hecht was operating ten stores in the Baltimore-Washington market. Its lone remaining New York store in Flushing was quickly put up for sale, and its Fell's Point stores were closed. The merger meant the closure of the former Hecht Brothers' stores at Baltimore and Pine Streets and at Howard and Franklin Streets. There was a tentative promise to maintain operations at the former Hub store at Baltimore and Charles Streets, but the centerpiece of the company was the former May Company store at Howard and Lexington Streets. Both Hecht and May officials promised, "The people of Baltimore are going to have an A-1, remodeled, up-to-date store at the prime location downtown. It will be the largest store and we hope the best in Baltimore."[50] The store received a complete makeover from top to bottom and took the new moniker of Hecht-May. Customers were encouraged to watch the daily progress at the new Hecht-May store, "destined to be the most complete, beautifully appointed, skillfully serviced store in all downtown." The store was designed to meet "the needs of every shopper regardless of wealth or tastes." On February 1, 1959, Hecht-May opened its doors as Baltimore's newest and largest department store. But Hecht family member Sandi Gerstung recalls that the Howard and Lexington Street store didn't feel like Hecht's at first: "It was a bigger store than the Baltimore Street store, but it didn't have quite the same family feel."

Just four months later, the company formally announced that it was abandoning its store at Baltimore and Charles Streets, the original Hub location. Downtown Baltimore did not need two Hecht Company stores. After sixty years of "friendly Maryland service," the Charles Street Hecht Company store took "its final bow" on June 29, 1959.

Hecht-May promised "fashion perfection at high frequency." The store promoted designer labels in its new Charles Room shop and fine dining in its Courtyard Restaurant, striving to become part of Baltimore's social and shopping fabric. Hecht-May had a lot of catching up to do. Although the

The downtown Washington Hecht Company store was located in the city's shopping core at Seventh and F Streets. By the 1970s, its surrounding area had declined, as had the structure. Hecht's relocated its downtown store to the Metro Center area in October 1985. The Baltimore and Washington Hecht stores operated as separate divisions until 1973. *Collection of the author.*

The Baltimore Hecht Company officially merged with the May Company on February 1, 1959, creating Hecht-May at Howard and Lexington Streets. *Collection of the author.*

downtown Hecht-May's annual sales grew from $13 million to $15 million, Hutzler's downtown store was still the market leader with $25 million in sales. Sandi Gerstung says, "The Courtyard Restaurant was very pretty, but it was never able to compete with Hutzler's." She recalls the store's unique Festival of Flowers. This annual tradition was presented every May as a "tribute to Mother and to Mother Nature." "It was absolutely gorgeous," says Gerstung. "We had the entire floor covered in flowers." The Baltimore Hecht Company stores also tried to match Hutzler's famous Occasion Extraordinaire sale with its own "Blue Chip Event." Every June, Hecht's Blue Chip Event promised quality merchandise that was "timely and wanted." The featured goods required approval by the store's Merchandise Board. But unlike Hutzler's, the savings at Hecht's was at least 25 percent off, instead of the 20 percent reduction offered during Hutzler's Occasion Extraordinaire. Blue Chip Events promised "no remnants, no broken assortments, no incomplete sizes, and all merchandise is the kind the store could be proud to offer." The Blue Chip Event did not rival the excitement and tradition of Hutzler's sale, but it gave shoppers a reason to take a second look at the new Hecht Company.

The Hecht Company opened a large branch at the Reisterstown Road Plaza on October 30, 1961. It was the last suburban store that the company developed for over a decade. The Plaza store was designed to vie for Washington-area customers with its Northwest Baltimore location.[51] The Hecht Company, along with its Thrift Centers and Auto Centers, appeared content to serve the more modest department store shoppers. But behind the scenes, the Hecht Company slowly strengthened its merchandise offerings, increased its charge account solicitations and carefully targeted new customers through special sales promotions.[52] The company began to "stress high fashion lines while it continued to promote long-time budget types."[53] By the 1970s, the Hecht Company had turned its image and sales figures around. Hutzler family member George Bernstein acknowledges Hecht's transformation at its Baltimore stores:

> *If you have a business that doesn't change, then somebody will run right by you. The Hecht Company ran right by [Hutzler's]. Hecht's did a better merchandising job and a better marketing job than Hutzler's. Hutzler's was marketing to the elite, Hecht's was marketing to the general public. When Hecht's began to expand, they positioned themselves from being the "cheapest store in town" to the store that appealed to the middle class.*

The Hecht Company presented its third annual Festival of Flowers in May 1963. This display celebrated the country of Colombia. *Special Collections, University of Maryland Libraries.*

The Hecht Company stores also had the backing and support of the powerful May Department Stores Company. With May's corporate help, the Hecht stores in Baltimore and Washington became more competitive. Executive Peter Rosenwald says, "Hecht's customer base was moderate, but the store became trendier because the whole May Company became trendier." In February 1973, May merged the buying and managerial operations of the Hecht stores in Baltimore and Washington. The consolidation was seen as a move to upgrade the Baltimore operation. The Baltimore division "lacked the merchandising flair, quality of goods, and more affluent customer" as enjoyed by Hecht's Washington stores.[54] The merger gave the Hecht Company stores more buying leverage, but it also took executive positions out of the downtown Baltimore store. According to Peter Rosenwald, the Washington Hecht stores sold double the volume of the Baltimore Hecht stores. "The Hecht Company in D.C. was run by henchmen," says Rosenwald. "They were good, smart merchants, but

The Hecht Company store at the Reisterstown Road Plaza in March 1962, after heavy tides, winds and snow battered East Coast communities. In October 1961, the Hecht Company became the first store to open at the new Plaza shopping center. *Special Collections, University of Maryland Libraries.*

they were rough and not cozy." Both Hecht divisions were fully merged in 1974.

Although the company's headquarters moved to Washington, the Hecht Company continued to invest in the Baltimore market. The downtown store was "glamorized" in 1973, and a modern elaborate branch was opened at the Golden Ring Mall in 1974. It was the first Hecht store to open in Baltimore in thirteen years. The Golden Ring store had a different feel than the other Baltimore Hecht stores. It was full of antiques and artwork that helped shed the company's budget image. Golden Ring was followed by a store at the Columbia Mall in August 1975. Hochschild, Kohn, during the previous February, had abandoned the Columbia location due to extremely poor sales. Hecht wanted the Columbia store to be "the latest example of the aggressive marketing

The Hecht Company opened a store at the Golden Ring Mall on September 30, 1974. It joined Stewart's and Montgomery Ward at Baltimore's first two-level enclosed mall. *Photograph by the author.*

Hecht's Security Square Mall location served as a replacement store for the company's aging Edmondson store in August 1979. *Photograph by the author.*

strategy adopted by the company, and its efforts to portray an image of a quality store with timeliness."[55]

The Columbia and Golden Ring Hecht Company stores were extremely successful stores for the company. The downtown store prevailed despite a challenging climate. The stores at the Plaza and Northwood aged poorly and were too big for their sales volumes. Edmondson fell victim to an area "that was in pretty bad shape." In early 1979, it became the first Baltimore Hecht Company store to close its doors. Operating downscale stores in declining areas was not part of the company's plan to update and upgrade its image. On April 30, 1978, the company officially changed its name from the Hecht Company to simply Hecht's. The name change was part of an effort to "reflect a more contemporary image" since the former name was "too traditional for the type of customer the store now seeks."[56] Hecht's was now the store to imitate and to beat as the retailing market entered the turbulent 1980s.

Stewart's

On the Wrong Side of the Street

S tewart & Co. entered Baltimore's department store field in March
1902. Billed as "Baltimore's Biggest, Best Store," Stewart's featured
"high-grade merchandise at popular prices." Its beautiful, classic
emporium was located directly opposite Hutzler's and Hochschild,
Kohn on Howard Street. However, Stewart's leaderhip was located in
New York City. The store promoted its "New York Connection," but
many Baltimoreans considered Stewart's an outsider that had trouble
understanding the styles and tastes of the local customer. Although it
was a quiet store that carried quality merchandise, no other department
store in Baltimore suffered from such a persistent identity crisis as
Stewart & Co.

Before there was Stewart's, there was Posner's. Brothers Elias and Samuel
Posner came to Baltimore and opened a small store on Lexington Street
in 1877. Posner's was a one-price store that quickly grew to encompass
sixty separate departments. On October 21, 1886, the *Baltimore American*
proclaimed Posner's "the largest retail dealer in the south" and a business
that could "stand among the great department stores in the United
States."[57] Although Elias passed away in February 1885, Samuel Posner
purchased land along Howard and Lexington Streets in 1893 with hopes of
constructing Baltimore's biggest palace department store. In 1899, Samuel
Posner announced his plans for a new store designed by architect Charles
Cassell. This ambitious business expansion was continually delayed, but
Posner's finally opened its palace store in April 1900. Upon opening, the

Posner Brothers business stated, "This store is the successful establishment it is because it always has executed its promises to the very letter. The great measure of confidence the people have reposed in it has never and will never be betrayed."

Unfortunately, the new Posner's store was a huge burden to Samuel and his company. Rumors quickly spread that Posner's was looking for a buyer. On December 29, 1901, Posner's was acquired by H.B. Claflin & Co., a wholesale dry goods business that owned several department stores throughout the country. Claflin's purchase of Posner's store "gave promise to the store's future and largely increased its chances of growth."[58] Samuel Posner was praised for running a business that attracted the attention of one of the country's largest dry goods houses. Posner was able to relieve himself of the financial burden and "retire with respect and esteem."[59]

The negotiator of the deal was a man named Louis Stewart. Stewart was born in rural Kentucky and spent eighteen years in the railroad industry. In 1893, he switched careers and assumed the leadership of Louisville's New York Store.[60] By the time Stewart left Louisville in 1900, the New York Store had been renamed the Stewart Dry Goods Company. Stewart's remained a Louisville retailing landmark for nine decades. Louis Stewart became president of Claflin's James McCreery & Co. store in New York but was summoned to Baltimore to negotiate the purchase of Posner's. He never lived in Baltimore and never intended to.

From January to March 1902, Posner's held a lengthy clearance sale. The new owners promised to bring in a new stock of spring goods that would "be the equal in every way to any assortment of merchandise shown by the most prestigious stores in New York." The *Baltimore Sun* extended its "best wishes and congratulate[d] the new owners upon the fortuitous circumstances upon which they enter our city." However, the *Baltimore Morning Herald* acknowledged that the purchase is "received with profound regret on the part of the people of this city."[61] Regardless, the new owners of the business officially opened the doors on March 17, 1902. The store was named Stewart & Co. in honor of the man who brokered the purchase of Posner's.

Although his daughter attended Johns Hopkins University, Stewart rarely visited Baltimore or the store. He actively ran New York's McCreery's, and business very occasionally brought him to town. Former buyer Don Alexander recalls only one story about an early visit to the store by Louis Stewart:

Stewart's

The bustling intersection of Howard and Lexington Streets in 1957, in front of the flagship Stewart & Co. store. *Special Collections, University of Maryland Libraries.*

There was a former employee named Marie Nagangaft who went to work at Stewart's at age fourteen. She had lied about her age. She worked in the warehouse well into her eighties. One day, Marie was working on the main floor, and Mr. Stewart stepped off the elevator. In those days, there was a wire system that ran along the ceiling and carried change up to the cashiers on the balcony. As Mr. Stewart turned the corner toward stationery, one of the copper containers opened up, and he was showered with pennies. Everybody got a big laugh about it, but you didn't hear any other stories about old Mr. Stewart.

H.B. Claflin Co. experienced its own financial demise in 1914, and two years later, Stewart & Co. became a founding member of Associated Dry Goods (ADG). Associated's stores included Lord & Taylor, William Hengerer Co. in Buffalo and Hahne & Co. in Newark. Associated

Dry Goods' resources provided the Baltimore market with new types of merchandise and strengthened the store's buying power. Former manager Edwina Smith says, "Associated Dry Goods was a well-directed company. We would make trips to various ADG offices and meet with buyers who would give us good direction. Members shared information from the other divisions, and it was extremely helpful." ADG also provided financial assistance to Stewart's to help modernize and expand its facilities. Smith says, "We had a better source of income than the other stores." Buyer Don Alexander saw the benefits of Stewart's affiliation with Associated Dry Goods. "Hutzler's was a fine store, but it didn't have the buying power of Stewart's. If a Stewart's buyer wanted a certain item, they could get it from an ADG representative in New York. Stewart's leadership wasn't local, but everybody who worked there was local," says Alexander.[62]

By 1937, more than two thousand Baltimoreans were employed by Stewart & Co. Annual sales approached $5 million, and it was the first department store in Baltimore to be air conditioned.[63] Its white palace structure on the northeast corner of Howard and Lexington Streets catered to Baltimore's carriage-trade shoppers. It was the only Baltimore department store that carried fine imported tablecloths that matched Kirk Silver's chrysanthemum pattern, as well as Stieff Silver's rose pattern. In its later years, Stewart's tried to set itself apart from the competition with its "phenomenal" Shop-at-Home Service. Customers simply called 727-6262 and had access to a staff of approximately thirty-five telephone operators who immediately processed phone orders. Don Alexander says, "Customers would call in a phone order, and the operator would call right down to the specific department. Customers didn't have to wait for a clerk to come to the phone. A phone order could be processed and put into delivery that day. That separated Stewart's from the competition." Alexander recalls getting seven to eight hundred phone orders from one single newspaper advertisement. Executive trainees frequently sat in on conversations between operators and customers and learned the selling benefits of this "phenomenal" service.

The Hutzler, Hecht, Hochschild, Kohn and Gutman families were well-known members of Baltimore's strong Jewish community. These families were visible in the community, and many of them were active members of their congregations. There was no Stewart retailing family that resided in Baltimore, and the store was viewed as the "Gentile store." A former employee agrees that Stewart's was famous in Baltimore because a Jewish family didn't run the store: "Stewart's was known as a place to shop when you wanted to get away from Jews. There were Jewish families behind all of the other stores. The name wasn't Jewish. There were anti-Semitic people who didn't want to deal with Jews."

Don Alexander feels, "The perception of Stewart's [by some Baltimoreans] was as erroneous as it could possibly be." The store had a religious goods department that carried a vast assortment of Bibles, Catholic missals, rosaries and beads. In addition to the large bells displayed outside the store at Christmastime that "rang out the message of goodwill," Stewart's always featured a crèche in one of its Christmas windows. "You had to do something more than Santa and Rudolph," says manager Edwina Smith. But Stewart's gift department also had a large collection of Judaica. Alexander recalls, "Our buyer had difficulty finding enough Jewish merchandise. We even did some direct importing from Israel. About one-third to one-half of Stewart's buying staff was Jewish."

Stewart's traditionally struggled to maintain its image as a store that served the Baltimore market sufficiently. Some shoppers complained, "Stewart's didn't get Baltimore" or "Stewart's always bought the wrong colors." Others simply stated, "Stewart's didn't have the look or the feel that I wanted" or "There wasn't anything bad about the store; I just didn't need them." The store did not have a large tearoom or restaurant that encouraged shopping and socializing. "Hutzler's had fashion shows running constantly. Stewart's couldn't do that," says Alexander. Hecht family member Sandy Gerstung adds, "Stewart's had a very different aura than the other stores. I never crossed the street. We didn't know anybody there." Some people felt the store was stuffy and old-fashioned, while others viewed it as elegant and friendly. Stewart's employees were proud of their store and saw one another as family members. Alexander says, "It was a fun store. Don't think that the employees felt they worked for a second-rate store. We knew we were just as good as the other stores." Buyer Susan Nehmsmann feels, "A lot of people thought that Hutzler's was the only store. It was a lot about perception."

When Hutzler's opened its tremendously successful Towson store in November 1952, Stewart's management knew a countermove was necessary. With downtown retail sales figures declining, the large stores realized that the future was in the suburbs. On February 8, 1955, Stewart's entered the suburbs in style when it opened its first branch store. Located

Overhead heat lamps keep models warm outside Stewart's in December 1960. *Special Collections, University of Maryland Libraries.*

Stewart & Co. opened its popular York Road store in February 1955. The internationally renowned architectural firm Raymond Loewy and Associates designed the interior and exterior of the store. *Collection of the author.*

on York Road at the city-county line, the store was designed by the famed Raymond Loewy architectural firm. Loewy was "the long-lived French-born engineer who left his mark on everything from 'streamlined' trains to the Carling Black Label beer can to the interior of Air Force One."[64] Unlike the downtown location, the York Road Stewart's featured a popular restaurant, which boasted a Chesapeake Bay theme. The restaurant was the perfect setting for fashion shows and breakfasts with Santa. "York Road [Stewart's] was the number one store as soon as it was built. It took off like gangbusters," says Alexander. The York Road Stewart's was located in the perfect trading area for traditional downtown Stewart's shoppers. Unlike Hochschild's Belevedere, located just down the street, Stewart's operated a complete full-line branch store. After its success on York Road, Stewart's sought the Pikesville area for its next branch. Hutzler's wanted to build a shopping center on the site of the family homestead, Pomona, located on Reisterstown Road and the Beltway, but the company could not get the proper zoning. As Hutzler's was trying to get a store into Pikesville, Stewart's was able to secure a location at the Reisterstown Road Plaza, just south of Pikesville. Pikesville was the center of Baltimore's strong Jewish demographic, and the gentile Stewart's store worked hard at serving the neighboring community. "The Reisterstown Road Stewart's catered to the Jewish clientele, and the majority of our employees there were Jewish," says former manager Edwina Smith. Buyer Don Alexander talks about the struggle to satisfy the store's new customer base at the Reisterstown Road store:

> *What sold downtown and at York Road did not sell at the Plaza. Customers were not happy with mundane merchandise. They wanted high-end, glitzy, colorful clothing. We were selling tons of gold and silver panty hose! It was a high-fashion store, and we did a hell of a job. But it took buyers a long time to realize and understand the customer.*

The Reisterstown Road Plaza Stewart's opened on March 14, 1962, and joined the Hecht Company as the Plaza's anchor stores. Its distinctive exterior was complemented by its beautiful interior, designed by Raymond Loewy & Associates. By the late 1960s, the Plaza branch became popular for its "Old-Fashioned Bargain Days" in July. "In those days, we didn't have sales all the time, like we do now. We had this one sale, and we'd dress up in old-fashioned costumes," says Edwina Smith. "We did some good business at the Plaza on Old-Fashioned Bargain Day during a very slow time of the year."

Associated Dry Goods attempted several times to reinvent its Stewart's stores in Baltimore. ADG brought in a revolving door of executives who confused their customers with new merchandise offerings and hurt employee morale with excessive demands. A former employee remembered how one executive team tried to increase sales figures at Stewart's:

> *One new management group came in and assigned all sales managers some very lofty goals for each of their departments. Several months later, all sales managers were invited to a dinner at the Prime Rib. Each manager took his assigned seat. If you met or exceeded your sales goal, you were served prime rib. If you didn't make your sales goal, you were served franks and beans. It was humiliating for everybody at the restaurant, including the wait staff.[65]*

The interior of Stewart's Reisterstown Road Plaza store was also designed by the Raymond Loewy firm. Stewart's Plaza store opened for business on January 2, 1962. *Special Collections, University of Maryland Libraries.*

The mall entrance to Stewart's Plaza store during a massive snowstorm in March 1962. A Read's Drug Store is seen on the right-hand side of the photograph. *Special Collections, University of Maryland Libraries*.

By the mid-1960s, Stewart's was suffering from management's decisions. Former executive Paul Rosenwald says, "Stewart's was very weak and had poor merchandising standards. It was a victim of poor standards." In 1968, the company opened an undersized, inadequately designed branch at Westview that never gained momentum. "Westview didn't have the high-priced merchandise," says Smith. "There were just certain things that we didn't carry there that we should have." A large branch at the Timonium Mall followed Westview in February 1971. Built on York Road, north of the Beltway, the Timonium branch hoped to mimic the success of the York Road Stewart's and banked on the promise that Charles Street would be extended north of the Beltway up to the new mall. The Charles Street extension never occurred, and the Timonium Stewart's never achieved its anticipated success. "The Timonium store was to be more upscale, but the area's customers didn't have the money because of tuition bills,

The interior of Stewart's York Road, as seen in December 1982. *Special Collections, University of Maryland Libraries.*

mortgages and car payments," says buyer Susan Nehmsmann. The last of the Stewart's branches opened at the Golden Ring Mall in Northeast Baltimore. The large mall also included Hecht Company and Montgomery Ward stores. Unlike the nearby Eastpoint locations of Hutzler's and Hochschild, Kohn, Stewart's offered "main floor merchandise" at Golden Ring, and sales started strong. The store catered to a cash customer. "They weren't interested in charge accounts," says Smith. "I think that they were just brought up that way."

From its locations in a struggling downtown to the small, awkward Westview branch to a working-class mall location to a stylish suburban branch that courted well-heeled shoppers, Stewart's did not have a consistent image. The store carried quality merchandise, but its corporate management team in New York wouldn't commit to a specific profile. "They wanted to make us Bloomingdale's, but they should have left us alone," says Smith. Like many department stores across the country, Stewart's was unable to capture the youth market. It played an old-fashioned, somewhat stuffy role "that just wasn't right" in Baltimore. By

The downtown Stewart's store at Howard and Lexington Streets in 1977, two years before the store's final closure. *Collection of the author.*

the mid-1970s, Stewart's was number four in sales out of Baltimore's four department stores. As columnist Jacques Kelly reflects on the downtown stores, he says, "Hutzler's, Hochschild's and Hecht's were always quite busy. Stewart's never seemed terribly busy."[66] In some ways, that was its blessing. In other ways, it was its curse.

And the Rest...

B y the 1880s, more than two hundred dry goods establishments were located in downtown Baltimore.[67] Dry goods stores generally carried fabrics, lace, ribbons and notions. Only a handful of those early establishments were able to expand their offerings and gradually evolve into modern department stores. Hutzler Brothers, Hochschild, Kohn & Co., Hecht Brothers, Bernheimer Brothers and Posner Brothers made the transition and developed their "departments," but there are other former dry goods houses that should not be forgotten.

In 1882, Thomas O'Neill set up a small linen shop on Charles Street. It grew into one of Baltimore's most elite carriage-trade retailers. Originally from County Cavan, Ireland, O'Neill was a staunch Catholic dressed in striped trousers and a long coat who would greet customers at the store's main entrance.[68] He expanded his original business at Charles and Lexington Streets by gradually acquiring adjacent properties. O'Neill is immortalized in Baltimore's history because of his actions during the Great Fire of 1904. He believed that prayer saved his store from the downtown inferno and was forever indebted to the Catholic Church. In 1954, the *Baltimore Sun* told the story of O'Neill and the Great Fire of February 7, 1904:

> *Areas of city blocks lay devastated, the Union Trust Company opposite the O'Neill store was a torch late at night when dynamiters told Mr. O'Neill they intended to raze his store, as they had done dozens of others, in an effort to halt the progress of the fire. Mr. O'Neill begged for time. He later related*

how he drove in a carriage rapidly to the Carmelite Convent at Biddle and Caroline Streets and, awakening the nuns, begged them to pray for the safety of his store. When he returned to it, he said, the wind had shifted and O'Neill's was saved.[69]

Another account embellished the story with details of O'Neill sprinkling holy water at the store's entrance.[70] Gil Sandler says that he fell in love with the story of O'Neill's: "You pray to God to shift the wind and the wind shifts?" O'Neill vowed then and there to never forget his faith or the loyalty of his employees. "He cared for three things: his business, his family, and the church."[71] When he passed away in 1919, he left his business to his employees in the form of stock options; he left his wife an annuity of $25,000; and he donated $300,000 to Loyola College for building purposes. Additionally, he provided funds for the creation of a hospital to be run by an order of nuns that would offer free care to those in need in a building not named after O'Neill (instead named Good Samaritan Hospital); and he designated $5 million for the creation of a new cathedral.[72] It was fifty years before Bishop Sebastian officially consecrated the Cathedral of Mary Our Queen on North Charles Street on October 13, 1959. Parishioner James Doran says, "The bishop fought the cathedral tooth and nail. We didn't need that cathedral. We already had the most historic cathedral in the country, and they couldn't break the will. But the cathedral is not self-supporting, and every parish in the diocese has to keep sending in funds."

In 1928, O'Neill & Company employees sold their stock to Hahn Department Stores, the forerunner of the Allied Stores department store group. Allied did not alter the appearance or merchandise offerings of O'Neill's. The department store had a loyal clientele who knew their salesladies as Miss Lily, Miss Rose or Miss Mary. With its wooden counters and wooden floors, it was an old-fashioned store that didn't change much over the years. Display worker Bob Eney recalls setting up one of the display windows while dealing with the challenges of the antiquated structure:

The floors of O'Neill's were so rickety, and I was in charge of putting a mannequin dressed in an Adele Simpson suit in the main window at Lexington and Charles. Just as I was putting the last piece of glass in place, I heard a noise. Before I knew it, the Adele Simpson suit crashed right through the window and landed in the intersection![73]

O'Neill's, a unit of Allied Stores, survived the Baltimore Fire of 1904 but didn't survive the Charles Center development. The store closed in December 1954. *Special Collections, University of Maryland Libraries.*

Eney also remembers the plentiful offerings of the old store: "You would go into the Charles Street entrance and there were bolts and bolts of fabrics. A lot of the ladies would bring their dressmakers in with them."

A number of shoppers and job seekers were offended by O'Neill's hiring policy that publicly stated that "non-Catholics need not apply." O'Neill's location, somewhat off the beaten path, was an obstruction to Baltimore's newly planned Charles Center. During the early development stages of the downtown complex, O'Neill's was unable to reach a lease agreement with the landlords of its four adjacent structures. On September 25, 1954, Allied Stores announced that O'Neill & Company would cease operations after Christmas. The business quietly closed its doors on December 27, 1954, and all accounts were transferred to Stewart & Co. The building sat vacant for over six years until construction of the twenty-two-acre Charles Center project began on January 5, 1961. O'Neill's was the first building to

O'Neill and Company, Inc.

announces

that it will be open on

Monday, December 27, 1954

9.45 a.m. to 6.00 p.m.

for

the last time

O'Neill's will be open Monday to allow our customers the opportunity to make exchanges as well as purchases. Exchanges of all Christmas merchandise will be completely taken care of at this time.

All transactions that are in process will be completed to your entire satisfaction. All merchandise now in:
- Shoe & Jewelry repair • Fur Storage • Alterations

may be picked up Monday at your convenience or it will be delivered to your home upon your request.

Charge Accounts: Arrangements have been made by O'Neill and Company to have all of its charge accounts placed in the care of Stewart and Company. Our customers may be assured of courteous, helpful service from this fine store.

When O'Neill & Co. closed its store on December 27, 1954, charge accounts were transferred to the neighboring Stewart & Co. store. *Collection of the author.*

be ceremoniously demolished by the "clam-bucket" operated by Mayor J. Harold Grady.[74]

The city's first full-fledged department store to open was also the city's first department store to close. Founded in 1852 as a small store near Lexington Market, Joel Gutman & Co. was a Eutaw Street shopping destination for over three-quarters of a century. Joel Gutman & Co. built Baltimore's first ornate palace store, with over thirty separate departments, on September 27, 1886. More than three thousand people waited in line for hours to experience the new impressive emporium that captivated Baltimore shoppers.[75] At the time of its opening, no other business in Baltimore was as complete or opulent. But when Hutzler Brothers opened its larger, more elaborate palace on Howard Street in 1888, Joel Gutman's popularity waned. Arthur Gutman, Joel's grandnephew, worked at the store toward the end of its business life. "It was *the* store of Baltimore. It was a wonderful store in its prime, but it was badly mismanaged," says Gutman. Joel Gutman passed away in 1892, and his wife, Bertha, took control of the store. Bertha was a powerful leader who championed the store's saleswomen. She was a "guide, philosopher, and friend" to her female workforce and established a resting room for "weary saleswomen without cost to them."[76] When Bertha died in 1912, the business was left to the couple's five daughters. (Joel and Bertha's eldest daughter, Ella, married Hutzler brother David, and the two families became intertwined in family and business.) As Lexington Market grew, stalls and vendors filled the area, and Eutaw Street became less appealing to the store's elite customer base. Some businesses tried to persuade Gutman's to leave Eutaw Street. Arthur Gutman recalls, "The enclave on Howard Street wanted Joel Gutman & Co. to move to where Read's Drug Store is located. But they didn't have the money to do it. As Lexington Market expanded, Gutman's became rather seedy. The market killed the store."[77]

The Great Depression started in 1929, and Joel Gutman & Co. was unable to compete and continue. On April 17, 1929, the company announced a $1 million "epoch-making" going-out-of-business sale. Arthur Gutman says, "They brought in a high-profile outfit that specialized in liquidation. If we had $1 million of inventory, we wouldn't have had to liquidate!" Over the next few months, customers came from everywhere to say goodbye, and Joel Gutman & Co. eventually closed on June 1, 1929.

When modern-day Baltimoreans think of Gutman's, they think of Julius Gutman & Co. or, as it was known in its later years, Brager-Gutman's. Julius Gutman was a "second or third cousin" of Joel Gutman, and both men came

Most of Baltimore's department stores were located within one block of the city's famous Lexington Market. Several sidewalk vendors and stalls lined Eutaw Street, effecting the image of higher-end stores such as Joel Gutman & Co. This photograph dates prior to 1949, when a massive fire destroyed the structure. Lexington Market is one of several public markets currently operating in Baltimore City. *Collection of the author.*

from Baden, Germany.[78] When Julius arrived in Baltimore, he began working for Joel. "Julius left Joel's business and started his own store," says Arthur Gutman. This angered Joel's family. "He was a carpetbagger!" Julius Gutman & Co. opened for business in 1877 at Lexington Street and Park Avenue and never moved from that location. Gutman's was Baltimore's popular-priced department store and proudly served the city's lower- to moderate-income customer. Julius Westheimer, the company's former president, said, "Gutman's never was the grandest store in Baltimore's once popular retail district. But popular with shoppers, it was indeed."[79] The store was located one block from the intersection of Howard and Lexington Streets. In 1930, a grand L-shaped building that defied its lower-market image was built on its original site. Gutman's was home to the city's very first escalator. A 1981

And the Rest...

AFTER SEVENTY SEVEN YEARS ON EUTAW ST.

JOEL GUTMAN AND CO.

LOCATED
ON EUTAW ST. BETWEEN
LEXINGTON FAYETTE STS

Store Closed

TO MAKE
PREPARATIONS for

Going Out of Business Sale

HELP WANTED
250 SALESLADIES
For all departments. Those having previous experience preferred but not necessary, apply in person, Eutaw Street entrance, Monday 10 A.M.

HELP WANTED
FLOORMAN and SALESMEN
For all departments. Those having previous experience preferred, but not necessary, apply in person, Lexington Street entrance, Monday 3 P.M.

ONE MILLION DOLLARS' WORTH OF HIGH-GRADE DEPENDABLE DEPARTMENT STORE MERCHANDISE, STORE FIXTURES, OFFICE FURNITURE AND STORE EQUIPMENT, ALL MUST BE SOLD IN A LIMITED TIME---IN THIS EPOCH-MAKING GOING-OUT-OF-BUSINESS SALE

STORE WILL BE CLOSED

ALL DAY MONDAY, APRIL 15th
ALL DAY TUESDAY, APRIL 16th

The Entire Stock Now In This Store and Our Two Warehouses Are Being Arranged and Marked Down!

Every resource at the command of the JOEL GUTMAN and COMPANY organization has been drawn upon to make this GOING-OUT-OF BUSINESS SALE the Supreme Selling Event of our Entire Business History covering more than Three Quarters of a Century on Eutaw Street.

The same salespeople that have served us and you for these many years, and to whom we can never be too grateful have loyally and interestedly entered into the labor which this tremendous sale involves. Department Managers, Buyers, Floor Superintendents, Office Personnel, Inspectors and the many employees in all the Service Departments, all are working with but one purpose: To be so prepared that every one who comes to this sale will find it easy to select, and easy to buy.

SALE BEGINS
WEDNESDAY MORNING
APRIL 17th, AT 9 O'CLOCK PROMPT

FOR FURTHER PARTICULARS, PRICES AND FULL DETAILS, SEE DOUBLE-PAGE ADVERTISEMENT IN THE EVENING SUN ON TUESDAY

THERE WILL BE CROWDS
Thousands will attend this Sale from every part of Baltimore and Maryland. It will be the epoch-making event in Baltimore's Mercantile History.

You'll Be Surprised

When You Read of This Sale on Tuesday
When You Attend This Sale on Wednesday
When You See This Mountain of Merchandise
When You See The Quality of Merchandise

A WORD TO OUR PATRONS
You who have known our store it's worthy merchandise—are especially urged to be here on Wednesday and to read from day to day the offerings of this Great Going-Out-of-Business Sale.

After seventy-seven years, Joel Gutman & Co. became the first Baltimore department store to cease operations. From April 17 to June 1, 1929, the company held a final liquidation sale at its Eutaw Street store. *Collection of the author.*

article in the *Baltimore News American* said, "The Depression was made for Julius Gutman's and Lexington Street, Baltimore's great thoroughfare of the cheap store, the five-and-dime and those places that were in a perpetual state of going out of business."

Gutman's had a long life in the Baltimore market and deserves to be acknowledged as one of Baltimore's main department stores. It carried merchandise that others didn't and served customers that others wouldn't. Bobbie Gutman, wife of store executive Henry Gutman, says:

> *I feel a little shunned when Gutman's is not seen as one of Baltimore's great stores. We certainly had a presence. Many people just want to hear about the carriage trade. You had so many choices as to where to shop downtown. You would go to the store that you depended on and the store where you knew everything was.*

In the 1940s, Gutman's introduced the Washington's Birthday Sale concept to Baltimore. The store began preparing for the extremely popular event the previous October and spent time acquiring samples and odd lots by the thousands. Henry Gutman remembers, "We had a George Washington Birthday Sale where we sold dollar bills for eighty-nine cents. It was a limited supply of maybe one hundred. Once we even offered an old beaten-up Chevy for one dollar. It was a functioning car!" Until the 1950s, the store operated on a cash-only basis. Gutman's slogan was "Pay Cash and Pay Less."

Gutman's longtime competitor was Brager-Eisenberg at Eutaw and Saratoga Streets. Albert Brager was a former business partner of Ferdinand Bernheimer but founded his own popular-priced store in 1882. Brager merged his store with Eisenberg's Underselling Store in 1929. Brager-Eisenberg's operated a successful thrift-oriented operation that was famous for the slogan "Before Buying Elsewhere, Say to Yourself, 'Wonder What It Costs at Brager-Eisenberg's.'" Both Brager-Eisenberg and Gutman's opened suburban stores in the 1950s, but they were very small and incomplete. Former Gutman president Julius Westheimer said, "The small stores were better than nothing, but they were not what they should have been." By 1959, both Brager's and Gutman's suffered declining sales. Henry Gutman says, "Brager-Eisenberg was in trouble and having difficulties." The two firms agreed to a merger on August 3, 1959. "The merger saved both stores," said Westheimer. Henry Gutman agrees: "Gutman's was minimally profitable and not even every year."

Julius Gutman & Co., along with Schulte-United, Woolworth, McCrory's and Read's Drug Stores, lined the south side of Lexington Street, between Park Avenue and Howard Street, in 1956. *Special Collections, University of Maryland Libraries.*

The combined firm moved into the Gutman building on Lexington Street. The Brager complex, a hodgepodge of buildings, was sold to Hochschild, Kohn and soon housed its relocated furniture store. Gutman's tall building was renovated in 1955 and was located more prominently than Brager's. Bobbie Gutman recalls, "Gutman's had a very popular and pleasant lunch counter, along with a dining room downstairs. But it wasn't anything special."

Harry Weinberg bought the Brager-Gutman building in 1964 and purchased the business in 1970. Weinberg amassed a collection of rundown buildings in downtown Baltimore and refused to spend money on their redevelopment. He had a strong, stubborn personality and was interested in running Brager-Gutman's. Executive and family member Henry Gutman stayed with Weinberg for a short time before he left the business. Gutman says about Weinberg, "He was crude and uneducated. He even kicked his

In 1976, Brager-Gutman's served as a retail anchor on the new Lexington Street pedestrian mall. *Special Collections, University of Maryland Libraries.*

father out of his own business! He was very difficult to work for. It was always his way or no way." When Gutman left Brager-Gutman's, he says that he never stepped foot in the store again. "There was no reason to. It really wasn't a pleasant business arrangement [with Weinberg]."[80]

Julius Westheimer, Julius Gutman's grandson, said, "Shoppers might go to Hutzler's or Hecht's for the good stuff, but they came to Gutman's to save a buck." The store did not carry high-fashion merchandise, although its Pretty Bird Shop, across the street from the store, tried to court younger, hip shoppers. But for fabrics, draperies and notions, many Baltimoreans went to Brager-Gutman's exclusively. Michael Mankovich, co-owner of Hampden Junque, recalls shopping at Brager-Gutman's almost exclusively as a youth. "They had this notions counter that must have been ten feet by ten feet that contained hundreds of items that cost four cents," says Mankovich. "There were bobby pins, hair clips, everything. Little kids spent hours just reaching through this crap." As a child, Mankovich preferred using the French pronounciation "Brah-zhay Goot-mahn" when referring to the store's name.

Washington's Woodward & Lothrop department store claimed the title of the first American department store to open branch locations. Founded as the Boston House in 1880, Woodward & Lothrop helped anchor Washington's F Street shopping district before it expanded into Richmond (September 1891) and Baltimore. Woodward & Lothrop opened a large retail store at the southeast corner of Park Avenue and Lexington Street on March 15, 1893. The four-story department store offered "high-class dry and fancy goods" and followed three business principles: "one-price only, qualities guaranteed the best and prices the lowest, and money refunded upon request, giving the purchaser the benefit of any or all competition."[81] The venture was short-lived. The company struggled to keep the various stores well stocked and well managed from its Washington headquarters. Reports state that "shipping and communication difficulties were responsible" for the downfall of its branches in Baltimore and Richmond.[82] Within a few months, Woodward & Lothrop announced that it was "going to retire from business in Baltimore," and the store permanently closed on December 30, 1893.

Another store that deserves mention is Schleisner Co. Schleisner's was not a department store but, rather, an exclusive designer ready-to-wear store. Solomon Schleisner founded his first store in 1906 on Lexington Street and moved to Howard and Clay Streets in 1921. In September 1931, it relocated to Howard and Saratoga Streets. In 1928, Schleisner's opened a branch in Salisbury that was eventually sold to his son-in-law Lewis Hess in 1950. Bobbie Gutman says, "You went to Hess for shoes. You went to Schleisner's for dresses, and you went to Hutzler's for everything else."[83] The Schleisner Co. expanded to Pikesville with its Suburban-West location in 1955. Although the "definitively Pikesville" store maintained its high-fashion profile, the company struggled with the burden of operating a small, specialized independent business. Business disagreements within the family did not help the company's longevity. On December 26, 1961, Schleisner's advertised "Everything We Own Downtown on Sale." The advertisement announced that the company was "going to have a bigger and better store." Unfortunately, that bigger and better store never came to be. Schleisner's quickly vacated its flagship store, and the building became a new home for Hahn Shoes. In March 1962, it held a "sale of unclaimed dresses," and by the end of the year, Schleisner's was just another lost Baltimore tradition.

Run Right to Read's

It would be unfair to talk about the intersection of Howard and Lexington Streets and not pay homage to the Read Drug & Chemical Company. Known simply as Read's, the company played an active role in the lives of Baltimoreans. With its flagship store located at the southeast corner of Howard and Lexington Streets, Read's became a household word as the company grew to ninety-nine locations by 1977.

Of course, Read's was not a department store, but as a drugstore and soda fountain, it served as a shopping and social destination, especially its main store. William H. Read founded the company in 1883 at the corner of Light and German Streets, but it moved to the intersection of Howard and Lexington Streets in 1889.[84] In 1899, Read sold his store to a competitor, Arthur Nattans, owner of the Superior Drug Company on Howard Street. It was Nattans who expanded the business to Oldtown, Broadway and many other city locations and developed the company's Wonder Store at the city's main shopping intersection. The four-level store, built during the height of the Depression, was "the largest construction project to be undertaken in the area for some time."[85] Read's newly rebuilt store opened on September 21, 1934, and contained a basement restaurant featuring live music by Lou Becker's orchestra from noon to 2:00 p.m., a balcony lunch counter, a photography studio, a large perfume bar, twenty-five telephone booths, an "up-to-the-minute" beauty salon, a cigar counter, a large fourth-floor commissary and, of course, "an unexcelled prescription department where a registered nurse who acts as the store mother is always in attendance."

The $200,000 purchase price was no small investment for the company. Grandson Joe Nattans recalls, "I do remember that my grandfather took a risk. He said, 'I'm going to go with it.' So he opened it up. It was a major attraction. Not only was it a really good store, it was a really popular store." Hutzler family member George Bernstein says, "Read's was always very interesting. It was a big store that sold all kinds of crap." Columnist Jacques Kelly feels that Read's "was like the toiletries department to the department stores. They were wildly competitive in price."

Its slogan "Run Right to Read's" dates back to the early twentieth century. After an August 1914 fire severely damaged the original Howard and Lexington Streets store, a bus from Curtis Bay posted a sign for another downtown Read's location at Liberty and Lexington Streets. This sign read "This Bus Runs Right to Read's," and this eventually became the company's slogan.[86] Baltimore and national celebrities frequented the main store. Meyer Caplan of Caplan Brothers Glass and Aaron Kaplan of the B&O Railroad were close friends and frequent customers of Read's. Joe Nattans recalls:

> They [Caplan and Kaplan] used to come to Read's two to three times a week and sit on the balcony for an extended lunch. They weren't just good customers, they were good buddies. They were very generous, never in a bad mood and were always giving out things, B&O tokens, Orioles tickets… they always had a pocketful of giveaways.[87]

By 1958, Read's had grown to fifty-eight locations throughout the Baltimore area and the Eastern Shore. The company never expanded beyond that immediate boundary and remained a Maryland corporation. Joe Nattans says, "We had an understanding that Peoples Drug and Drug Fair would not come into Baltimore as long as we didn't come into Washington." By the mid-1970s, the company that was famous for its cinnamon sticks and Hendler's ice cream was unable to compete successfully. Arthur Nattans's trust stated that his descendants would inherit the stock after he passed away. "We could have kept it going, but five of the seven descendants were not active in the business," says Joe Nattans.[88] In early 1977, Rite Aid purchased Read's Drug Store, promising that it wouldn't make dramatic changes. Rite Aid soon turned on its agreement. "Rite Aid promised to keep the name and the soda fountains and they didn't," says Nattans. "Rite Aid wanted everybody to take a lie detector test and ended up installing hidden microphones that were monitored by the chief of security." By November 1977, Rite Aid had dismantled the popular lunch counter at the Howard and Lexington Streets

The flagship Read's Drug Store as seen during the 1964 Christmas shopping season. By 1964, the crowds of shoppers had significantly dropped in size. *Special Collections, University of Maryland Libraries.*

store. Customers could no longer "Run Right to Read's," and Baltimoreans had one less reason to spend an afternoon downtown.

Read's lunch counter was a convenient stop for many Baltimore shoppers who preferred it to the department store restaurants. Several restaurants and cafeterias served downtown customers. Oriole Cafeterias were a popular dining option. Founded by Herbert Dunnock in 1922, Oriole Cafeteria opened its first full-scale cafeteria on Light Street before expanding to locations on Howard Street and North Avenue. The Cafeteria promoted inexpensive Maryland cuisine. Restaurateur Alan Katz says that Oriole's downfall in 1975 was due to the company's inability to make necessary operational changes. "Owner Reg Dunnock didn't change Oriole too much. You can't make any money if you don't change," says Katz.

Alan Katz ran the popular White Coffee Pot restaurant chain, another Baltimore institution. White Coffee Pot was founded in 1931 when Alan's parents, Miles and Betty Katz, purchased three financially troubled downtown restaurants at Charles and Oliver Streets, Howard and Franklin Streets and on North Avenue. Katz says, "My father said the owner of the restaurants would give him the three restaurants if my father paid the purveyor's bills. When I took over, my father told me that I didn't have to make any money as long as I didn't lose any money!"[89] White Coffee Pot expanded beyond downtown and established restaurants in many of the city's new shopping centers. Soon the company changed its name to White Coffee Pot Inns and entered the catering business. "We had the best soups and the best hot cakes," says Katz. "Our problem was that we never priced our food where it should have been." In 1993, Katz sold his final White Coffee Pot and concentrated on his other restaurant operations.

If there ever was an affordable downtown social dining destination, it was Horn & Horn. Many shoppers, especially from Charles Street, ventured from the retail district for a meal at Horn & Horn. The family that founded Baltimore's Horn & Horn restaurant and cafeteria also founded the popular Horn & Hardart Automat chain in Philadelphia and New York. In 1891, brothers Frank, George and Joseph Horn entered the restaurant business in Baltimore, but there was contention about the menu; George wanted to offer more seafood, and Joseph disagreed. As a result, Joseph left Baltimore and partnered with Frank Hardart in Philadelphia.[90] Philadelphia's Horn & Hardart shared many of the same recipes with Horn & Horn, but Baltimoreans were extremely partial to their hometown eating place. Jacques Kelly comments, "Horn & Hardart was horseshit. It was like they had a machine that took the taste out."[91]

Baltimore's Horn & Horn specialized in dishes such as chicken biscuits and oyster potpies but offered a lot more than just food. "Everybody came together at Horn & Horn," says historian Gil Sandler. "The waitresses never carried pads." The all-night Baltimore Street restaurant served good, wholesome, cheap food to "every person who ever walked the streets of Baltimore," says Carl Horn. He recalls some of Horn & Horn's most well-known figures:

> *Governor McKeldin always went up to the counter and gave out pencils. He would usually wear a black-eyed susan, one of his favorite flowers. He would just come through and talk to everybody. William Donald Schaefer was also a regular at the counter. Horn & Horn catered to mayors and politicians, as well as burlesque dancers from the Block.*

In July 1959, the Katz family of White Coffee Pot fame boldly purchased Baltimore's legendary Horn & Horn restaurant on Baltimore Street. Alan Katz expanded the Horn & Horn name to cafeterias and "smorgasbords"

The *Horn & Horn* tradition since 1891

Innovation has always been welcome at Horn & Horn. This newest Horn & Horn Cafeteria presents the very latest in decor and facilities to assure dining convenience and comfort. We are, however, old-fashioned about our standards of quality. Through the years we created and tested a great variety of recipes. These time-tested recipes help explain why patrons since 1891 prefer our Maryland cooking . . . our own baked pies and cakes . . . and our other specialties that are uniquely Horn & Horn. Come in and enjoy a delicious dining experience. Bring the family. Children specials are featured daily.

During the gay nineties, Horn & Horn created recipes of unusual merit and baked its own sweet goods. These same unique recipes are equally delightful to this day. Horn & Horn offers its own baked cakes and pies . . . its own delectable specialties.

Baltimore in the gay nineties when *Horn & Horn* first opened its doors.

Founded in 1891, Horn & Horn was a Baltimore Street dining institution whose family members also operated Horn & Hardart establishments in Philadelphia and New York City. Horn & Horn also operated a competing restaurant in the 1920s on Horn & Hardart's home turf in Philadelphia. Unlike Horn & Hardart, Baltimore's Horn & Horn did not house a coin-operated Automat. By the 1970s, Horn & Horn had established cafeterias and smorgasbords in many of the region's most popular shopping centers. *Collection of the author.*

in Baltimore's suburbs. Carl Horn, a grandson of the founder, was always available to keep up "the Horn & Horn standard" by either tasting recipes or keeping the restaurants clean. Over the years, Horn's shortened its hours and lost its prominence, much like Howard Street's department stores. In January 1977, the beloved original Horn & Horn closed its Baltimore Street doors. The company's suburban cafeterias and smorgasbords lingered into the 1990s.

The lunch counters at Read's, White Coffee Pot and Horn & Horn did not compete with Howard Street's department stores—they complemented them. Unfortunately, the department stores and the lunch counters were not immune to the economic challenges that faced downtown businesses across the country.

Santa Claus Is
Coming to Town

For many Baltimoreans, a trip to the downtown department stores was an annual Christmas ritual. People came to shop, celebrate and dream. Toy departments were expanded to accommodate children's wishes. Annual holiday events were established, and Santa Claus made appearances. Special animated figures and brilliant designs were showcased in the store windows. While Hutzler's and Hochschild, Kohn battled for the unstated title of Baltimore's True Home of Christmas, all the department stores competed for customers, each offering holiday enticements and personal traditions.

Baltimore's department stores invested in elaborate holiday windows as early as the 1920s, enticing people to shop inside. By the 1950s, many American department stores spent 60 percent of their annual window budgets solely on their Christmas windows.[92] Following this trend, Baltimore displays grew more ornate every year, and many holiday windows were planned a year in advance. Hochschild, Kohn recruited design talent from internship programs associated with institutions like the Maryland Institute College of Art.[93] O'Neill's and Stewart & Co. courted customers with Christmas display windows of religious Nativity scenes showing Christ in the manger.

Stewart's featured a fifty-voice employee choir at holiday time. Starting in 1928, the employees, dressed in vestments, sang carols from the store's southern staircase daily. For many years, the choir was featured daily on WFBR radio. Led by Mrs. Louis Spencer of

Crowds gather to watch the animated holiday figures at the May Company store on Howard Street. *Courtesy of Jacques Kelly.*

Stewart's always featured a crèche among its holiday window displays. *Special Collections, University of Maryland Libraries.*

A display of carolers is mounted along the side of the downtown Hochschild, Kohn store in 1959. *Collection of the author.*

the Peabody Conservatory, the choir helped "spread the traditional Christmas spirit of Peace on Earth, Good Will Toward Men." Stewart's was also recognized for its large Christmas bells that "rang the message of good will" outside its doors.

Hochschild, Kohn and Hutzler's competed intensely at Christmastime. From 1936 to 1966, Hochschild's presented its Toytown Parade on Thanksgiving Day. The parade started at the Art Museum and wound its way through the city's streets, ending at Hochschild's front door at Howard and Lexington Streets. Store employees, alongside hired students from Johns Hopkins University, helped man numerous cloth balloons rented from a New York firm. The balloons would arrive in Baltimore on Thanksgiving Eve and were quickly inflated by vacuum cleaners on Thanksgiving morning. At the parade's peak, more than 250,000 people lined the route to see the balloons and hear the bands.

at 9.30 Thanksgiving Morning!

BALTIMORE'S FIRST, GIGANTIC

TOYTOWN PARADE
SEE!!!

Giants! Huge Dragons! Noah's Ark! Clowns! FUN! STIRRING MUSIC!

THROUGH THE HEART OF THE CITY

Start— Charles St. and University
Parkway at 9.30 A. M.
South on Charles to 21st
East on 21st to St. Paul
South on St. Paul to Mt. Royal
West on Mt. Royal to Cathedral
South on Cathedral to Read
West on Read to Howard
South on Howard to H. K. & Co.

presented Thanksgiving Morning by

HOCHSCHILD. KOHN & CO.

Hochschild, Kohn & Co. inaugurated its first Toytown Parade on Thanksgiving Day 1936. The parade was a beloved Baltimore tradition for thirty years. *Collection of the author.*

A 1945 photograph of Hochschild, Kohn's Toytown Parade, looking north up Howard Street from Lexington Street. This photograph shows one of the parade's signature "grotesque and occasionally terrifying giant, rubberized figures." Store employees, dressed as clowns, escorted the balloons. *Courtesy of the Jewish Museum of Maryland.*

Hochschild's Toytown Parade was more modest than Macy's Parade in New York, Gimbels Parade in Philadelphia or Hudson's Parade in Detroit. Columnist Jacques Kelly comments, "The Toytown Parade was not trying to be the Macy's Parade. That was all part of its honesty." Hochschild's sales promotion manager, B. Lewis Posen, conceived the event, but the first parade almost didn't happen. Traveling from New York to Baltimore the day before Thanksgiving, the balloons were delayed by a massive snowstorm. State police in Pennsylvania and Maryland helped locate and reroute the trucks safely to Baltimore. The balloons arrived fourteen hours behind schedule, but an army of twenty vacuum cleaners was ready for quick inflation.[94]

Santa Claus and his team of helpers always arrived on the parade's final float and signaled the start of Baltimore's Christmas season. Along the parade route, Santa's helpers busily collected children's wish lists. Santa answered

Left: A close-up of the "real" Laughing Santa on a Toytown Parade float in 1948. *Collection of the author*.

Below: Hochschild's famous Laughing Santa is joined by Mrs. Claus in the store's Lexington Street window. This photograph dates from 1941. *Collection of the author*.

every letter that had a name and return address. In 1941, Hochschild's installed its famous Laughing Santa in the store's Lexington Street window. Joined by Mrs. Claus, Santa held a storybook and let out a loud and hearty laugh each time he turned a page. The store stated, "The Laughing Santa Claus is the symbol of Christmas spirit at Hochschild, Kohn's." It remained true until the mid-1960s.

By the 1960s, suburban expansion of the department stores diminished the allure of downtown Christmas shopping. Shopping malls focused on displays and events and became the new model for Christmas shoppers.[95] As downtown business deteriorated, the stores' commitment and investment in holiday decorations also faded. In 1967, Bob Eney joined Hochschild, Kohn as its visual merchandising manager. Bob assumed the role of "the man who killed the Toytown Parade." Eney explains, "Martin Kohn wanted out of the parade. When I came on board, he asked me about my opinion of the parade. I told him that I was embarrassed by it. If I could use the money that was spent on the parade, I'd spend it on stuff for the windows."[96] Eney called the parade "ragtag," and it was exactly what Kohn wanted to hear. In July 1967, Hochschild, Kohn announced the cancellation of the Toytown Parade. Store officials said, "The quality [of the balloons] do not meet a standard which we feel should be maintained for a very loyal Baltimore public."[97] Countless Baltimoreans were outraged, but sadly, many of Baltimore's storied holiday traditions disappeared as downtown business declined.

Penguins and Hochschild, Kohn were strangely synonymous. The very first mascot of the Toytown Parade was a penguin, and Hochschild's usually devoted one of its windows to a live penguin display. This promotion was so successful that twelve live Cape Jackass penguins were kept year-round in a window at the Eastpoint Mall store. The store partnered with the Baltimore Zoo, which oversaw the proper care of the animals. Kohn family member Liz Moser recalls the penguins as "good advertisements. They were a very good ploy to get children to look at the windows. The penguins were just great excitement." Employee Pat Leibowitz adds, "Hochschild's had a little car that took people from store to store. But that car also had a schedule to take care of the penguins. The penguins were a gimmick, and we needed gimmicks." The Eastpoint Mall store even named its in-store restaurant the Penguin Room, complete with penguin-shaped ice cream treats for the children.

Hutzler's was one of Baltimore's favorite stops for Christmas. The store's slogan, "A Gift from Hutzler's Means More," was never more significant

The main selling floor of the downtown Hecht-May store, proclaiming the business as "The Store of the Christmas Spirit." *Special Collections, University of Maryland Libraries.*

than at Christmastime. Even after the holiday, many people returned unwanted presents by placing them in Hutzler's boxes. "Our return policy was as liberal as one could be," says Hutzler family member George Bernstein. "If it was something that we sold, we'd take it back. We bent over backward for customers, and rightfully so." Hutzler's offered personal shopping services long before such things became standard practice in many large stores. The store's Gift Advisory Bureau advertised, "Let us take over your Christmas shopping because we have a gift for doing it." Hutzler's was the home of Breakfast with Santa in the Colonial Restaurant and Trainville in the store's Toytown Annex on Eutaw Street. When people reminisce about Christmas at Hutzler's, they recall the elaborate windows. Hutzler's had eight prominent display windows along its Howard Street front, and children clamored to see the exhibits. Advertising manager Sandy Schmidt admits, "We never had mechanical windows at Hutzler's. Those were next store at Hochschild's."

Looking north up Howard Street during a rainy December day in the late 1960s. *Special Collections, University of Maryland Libraries.*

In 1976, Howard Street retailers spent $50,000 trying to bring decorations and shopping excitement back to the deteriorating shopping area. Merchants wanted to promote Howard Street as "the area's biggest and most accessible shopping place" since it was the only "center" that housed all four big stores. *Special Collections, University of Maryland Libraries.*

In the 1980s, Hutzler's was best known as the home of the talking reindeer, Tinsel and Beau. Tinsel and Beau were introduced at Hutzler's Towson store in 1978 and replicated at all locations the following year. Tinsel and Beau lived in a hut with only their front halves exposed to the public. Children lined up to see and talk to the reindeer, which always moved their heads and responded. Behind the scenes, a person looked at the children through a peephole and operated the reindeer's movements by squeezing handles. Although they only appeared at the Howard Street store for 1979 and 1980, Tinsel and Beau were a chainwide tradition until the store's final Christmas.

Shirley Brewer was one of the Tinsel and Beau voices at Hutzler's Southdale in 1982. She attended Reindeer Training School, which was held in an attic at the old Howard Street store. There were no written instructions, but she was told that the reindeer couldn't talk about religion or politics. "What kid is going to talk politics?" thought Brewer. The trainees practiced with the controls and handles that made the reindeer move. The session was easier than the first day on the job. "The kids would come up one after the other, and you had to always think about what you were going to say. You didn't want the kids to hate reindeer for the rest of their lives," says Brewer.

Shirley Brewer poses in front of the talking reindeer, Tinsel and Beau, at the Southdale Hutzler's in 1982. Brewer served as one of the voices of Tinsel and Beau for the holiday season. When the reindeer weren't chatting with visitors, they wore blindfolds while signs stated that "Tinsel & Beau were napping." *Courtesy of Shirley Brewer.*

Tinsel was a girl and Beau was a boy, and the operator used two voices to differentiate between the two deer. Brewer learned to recite "'Twas the Night Before Christmas" using both voices of the reindeer. One day, the store was pretty empty, and she decided to practice the poem. Brewer remembers, "All of a sudden, a clerk, with her arms folded, stood in front of my peephole and said, 'Will you please be quiet! You haven't stopped talking since you started!' The clerk dampened my mood, but I realized that she was a miserable person."

Brewer had friends who asked her to "do her reindeer voices." She couldn't. "I had to be in the hut. Once I got into the hut, I put everything out of my head and felt the part." After vocalizing for Tinsel and Beau, Brewer feels differently when she sees other deer or "kin." "I take it personally when I see a deer after it was hunted or if I see a head mounted on a wall. It upsets me. It's like seeing a relative." Brewer worked as a speech therapist when she moonlighted as the voice of Tinsel and Beau at the Southdale Hutzler's. "It was a great way to connect with children. Kids would just open up their hearts and just talk," says Brewer. "I put a lot of myself into it. It was a really special job."

White Sale

Traditionally, department stores were designed to give white middle-class women a place to shop, browse, linger and dine. They were businesses that brought special merchandise and special events to well-heeled women who could afford to spend the day "on the town." However, very few American department stores followed an open-door policy, and people of color were generally not welcome. Black shoppers at Wanamaker's in Philadelphia were always followed and asked, "Will you be purchasing that item?" They were never seen above the basement level at Boston's Filene's specialty store, and they drank out of separate drinking fountains at Wanamaker's in Wilmington, Delaware. Even in New York City, a 1948 survey of shoppers showed that 21 percent of white customers did not want Negro salespersons handling their clothing, lingerie or food.[98]

Baltimore can be seen as the "northernmost urban outpost of segregationist culture," and these discriminations were especially true in Baltimore's department stores, arguably the city's most prominent businesses.[99] These stores created a form of utopia for white shoppers and, through their segregationist policies, helped "put racism on display."[100] Many middle-class white shoppers had African Americans working for them as hired help at their homes. These shoppers did not want to try on the same clothing as blacks, nor did they want to eat in the same dining rooms. The white department store customer simply saw herself as higher class than her black counterpart, which was indicative of her upbringing and social education.

Many people accepted segregation as a way of life, for whatever reason. Restaurateur Alan Katz says he "never thought anything about it [segregation]." When he started working for his family's White Coffee Pot coffee shops in 1954, no restaurants served African Americans. "They ordered carryout," says Katz. Not only was Joel Gutman & Co. the city's first department store, but it was also the first department store that hired a black manager. Arthur Gutman recalls the small restaurant located on a subterranean level between the main store and the annex and the man who ran it. "Gutman's was a pioneer because it had a restaurant that was managed by a black man. We were way ahead of our time. After we closed [in 1929], he became a popular caterer."

Despite this isolated anecdote, African Americans were generally denied service at the lunch counters, and they were not allowed to shop on the main and upper floors of the department stores. Many stores did not permit them to try on clothes. Hochschild, Kohn marked "FINAL SALE" on the purchase receipts of black customers.

In March 1930, the *Baltimore Afro-American* newspaper ran an article about enforcement of Baltimore department stores' "anti-Negro policy." The paper stated that Baltimore's department stores had recently "withdrawn the accounts of colored patrons" and "refused any sales to Negro customers." According to the report, the anti-Negro policy was initiated by O'Neill's and was quickly adopted by Hutzler's, women's clothier Bonwit Lennon and Hochschild, Kohn.[101] The paper sharply criticized the takeover of Bernheimer-Leader Stores by the May Company. It reported, "Bernheimer's, for years known as one of the cheapest in the city, built itself up upon colored trade, and eventually sold out to the May Company, which immediately inaugurated the policy of discouraging colored buyers." The *Afro-American* continued its attack on the May Company in an editorial from 1949:

> *To make a purchase at the May Company, a colored customer must either have a slip from your madam or be an employee of the store. The May Company in Baltimore has said time and time again that it does not want colored trade. It has no great heart for colored people. It has no deep belief in the people in this area. It was glad to get the dollars of colored people in 1927 and it used them to build itself into a big store which is now "Jim Crow."[102]*

Even ten years later, in 1959, the discriminatory policies persisted. A former African American customer tells her story about shopping at the downtown Hecht-May store:

My family had just moved to Baltimore from New York, and I was on the first floor of the Hecht-May store browsing. A security guard came up to me and asked me what I was doing there. I said that I was just looking. He said that I either had to shop in the basement or have a note allowing you to be on the street floor. I thought he was kidding, and before I knew it, I was in handcuffs and taken to a store security office. I was young, and I was allowed to make a phone call. I called my mother and told her exactly what happened. She told me, "You should have known better than to shop on a main floor in a Baltimore department store!"

Bob Eney worked in the visual merchandising department at Hochschild, Kohn. He recalls an event that occurred in the downtown store's hat department:

When I was at Hochschild, Kohn, Miss Maxine was the buyer for women's hats. One day, I was on the second floor and I heard her screaming. I went to look and saw this poor little black lady holding a hat above her head. Miss Maxine yelled at her, "Put that down! You can't go trying on those hats!" The lady said that she hadn't put it on her head. I didn't know that that was happening. It was horrible.

At Hutzler's, every black employee wore a uniform, since blacks were only employed as porters, housekeepers, food-service workers and elevator operators. Store president Albert Hutzler Sr. tried to uphold the Enoch Pratt Free Library's policy of not hiring black employees. As the library's chairman of the board, he told authorities in 1944 that he did not even hire blacks at his family's department store.[103] Hutzler's segregation policy even spilled over into its scouting department. Columnist Jacques Kelly says, "Hutzler's carried the Boy Scout line, and their National Council demanded that if a black Boy Scout came into a store, he could try on a uniform. Hutzler's ended up moving the entire Boy Scout department to Toytown on Eutaw Street. It was as far away as you could get from the main store."

Northwood was one of the city's first planned shopping centers and initially opened for business in 1938. The same real estate company that designed Roland Park developed the complex, and it was located five miles northeast of downtown Baltimore. Northwood was also adjacent to Morgan State College (now Morgan State University), a historically black college. Over the years, the center was rebuilt and included a Food Fair supermarket, a Read's Drug Store, an S.S. Kresge variety store, a movie theater and a Hecht Company department store, in addition to many other retailers. Black students were traditionally refused service at many of these businesses. One such business was the lunch counter at Read's Drug Store. On January 20, 1955, a group of student activists from Morgan State traveled to the flagship Read's at Howard and Lexington Streets. Frustrated by their inability to receive service at the Northwood Read's Drug Store, the students staged a sit-in demonstration with the help of the local chapter of the Committee on Racial Equality. After only two hours of peaceful demonstration at the downtown store, Read's announced, "We will serve all customers throughout our entire stores, including the fountains, and this becomes effective immediately."[104] This successful demonstration predated the famous Greensboro, North Carolina Woolworth sit-in by five years. In 1960, tensions continued at Northwood Shopping Center, especially at the segregated movie theater.

Baltimore's department store tearooms and lunch counters were the next targets of demonstrations. The Rooftop Restaurant at the Hecht Company store was a site of unrest. On March 20, four sit-in protestors were arrested at the restaurant for unlawful entry. At the initial hearing, the defending lawyers said, "Our major premise is that even if the Hecht Company has the right to keep people out because of their race, as the law is not constituted, the State is prohibited under the Fourteenth Amendment to use its power to arrest through the Police Department." The arrests did not deter the Morgan State students. On March 26, four busloads of protestors traveled to the four downtown department stores, intending to enter their eating establishments. The demonstrators had the support of the NAACP, which backed the group with legal assistance, transportation and bail money. The protestors did not target Brager-Gutman's since it had a long-standing practice of serving blacks on its sales floor and in its restaurant. "[Brager-Gutman's] had a lot of middle-class folks, but we had no problem serving blacks," says executive Henry Gutman.

Upon learning of the impending protest, Hochschild, Kohn executives Louis Kohn, Martin Kohn and Walter Sondheim Jr. called a meeting in the store's Continental Tea Room. Former executive Dick Wyman recalls:

> We gathered all of the waitresses, who were all white. We told them that we were going to integrate and that anybody could leave and we'd help them find new work. On the day of the march, the protestors were ready for a sit-in [at Hochschild, Kohn], and we just served them. It was something that Louis, Martin and Walter could take great pleasure in.

Unfortunately, Hutzler's, Hecht-May and Stewart's did not follow suit. These stores quickly closed their restaurants to all patrons. Media took notice of Hochschild, Kohn's new policy. Many customers applauded Hochschild's decision, but several chastised the store. The controversy is evident in many of the letters kept on file at the Maryland Historical Society:

> *I am writing to applaud your very sensible and forth-right stand, in deciding to serve all well-behaved customers, regardless of race, in your restaurant. You certainly may be assured that whatever department store purchases I make in the future will be at Hochschild's, and I shall try to persuade my friends to limit their buying to your store, also.* [Unsigned]

> *I like to congratulate you to stand with regards to desegregation of lunch counters. I believe it to be immoral, unethical, and undemocratic to have citizens of first and second-class. We need more civic-minded leaders like you. Very sincerely yours, John W.*

> *I want to commend you on the stand which you have taken. I am sure that members of our race will uphold their dignity and let you know that we* [blacks] *aren't the worst race in the world. Georgine E.*

> *I wish to protest the integration of your restaurants. Last Wednesday, I had a "smelly" Negro alongside of me that ended my lunch. It is regrettable that a store of first class merchandise should choose now to run a second-class restaurant. Consider me an ex-customer. Mrs. Joseph D.*

> *How could you! Who wants to sit in an eating place with a Negro? I think you are going to feel it very much. You are showing why we need another man like Hitler.* [Unsigned]

Letters of support outweighed letters of indignation. Hochschild's lost some credit customers—its greatest fear—but gained others. The integration policy at Hochschild's pressured the other stores to react likewise.

On April 16, 1960, Hutzler's quietly lifted its ban on serving black customers in its restaurants. Albert D. Hutzler III says, "The attitude of the family was that we should have served them long ago," although his grandfather was the least enthusiastic member of the family regarding integration. Upon hearing the news from Hutzler's, Hecht-May also lifted its ban. Hecht-May general manager Geoffrey Swaebe said, "If Hutzler's is now admitting Negroes, we will also." Stewart's was the last store to integrate its restaurant, the Georgian Tea Room. After the department store restaurants were integrated, the other departments of the stores soon followed. Martin Kohn's daughter Liz Moser says, "Blacks entered the workforce [at Hochschild, Kohn] at the sales level the same time the lunch counter was integrated. The changeover was total, complete and long overdue."

Integration also followed in the sales force. Back in 1956, *Fortune* magazine had reported that "Negro purchasing power cannot be overlooked in the economy of [Baltimore] or any other city if downtown shopping is to be maintained." By the mid-1960s, Baltimore stores began to reinvent their customer base, and stores like Hutzler's used black models occasionally in their advertising, welcoming new black customers.

On April 4, 1968, Reverend Martin Luther King Jr. was senselessly gunned down at a motel in Memphis, Tennessee. Reverend King was an advocate of nonviolent demonstrations that promoted equality. His death sparked outrage, and a number of American cities, including Baltimore, fell victim to heavy rioting. The Baltimore disturbance began on the 500 block of North Gay Street. Over four days, five people died, 2,200 arrests were made, three thousand people were injured and over four thousand fires burned East and West Baltimore. State policemen cordoned off the main shopping area bounded by Howard, Calvert, Baltimore and Franklin Streets to protect downtown. It was just a "precautionary move," but several merchants guarded their stores with rifles.[105] The department stores either drew their curtains or boarded up their show windows.

The rioting subsided after four days, but the perception of the city was forever changed. The net worth of stores like Hutzler's was invested in the real estate. Within two years, the value of Howard Street's land area plummeted as much as 80 percent. Middle-class residents quickly fled the city core. The suburban shopping centers offered free parking, late hours and specialized competition. There was no need for shoppers to make special pilgrimages to the downtown stores. Value and convenience, along with safety, became the mode of operation. Hutzler's in Towson became a stronger store than its Howard Street location. Stewart's did well on York Road, and Hecht Company enjoyed strong sales at Reisterstown Road Plaza.

Gil Sandler reflects on the department stores' strategy of investing in the suburbs rather than their traditional downtown flagship locations. "The stores ran away from the African American community," says Sandler. "What do you think Hochschild, Kohn was doing when it opened its branch stores? Do you think that it was just to take on an adventure?" Although many

in respect for the memory

of the late

Dr. Martin Luther King, Jr.

citizen, peacemaker,

champion of human rights

HUTZLER'S

Downtown Towson Eastpoint Westview Southdale

will be closed

MONDAY, April 8, 1968

All of Baltimore's department stores paid tribute to Martin Luther King Jr. at the time of his death and closed their stores on April 8, 1968. However, by that time, rioting had already broken out within many sections of East and West Baltimore. *Collection of the author.*

Baltimoreans wanted to see their city healed from the racial and economic struggles, a number of citizens simply left. "History will show people voted with their feet," says Sandler. "Whatever dialogue and nobility there was with the movements, what did the people do in the end?"

Close Out

B y the mid-1970s, Baltimore's downtown was a shadow of its former self. Residents and smaller businesses fled the city's inner core, leaving the remains of a faded shopping district. The *Baltimore Sun* criticized the stores for their "creaky wooden floors, obsolete bell systems, empty cafeterias, and invisible salespersons."[106] Baltimore focused its retail development at the city's Inner Harbor area as Howard and Lexington Streets crumbled. Sales at the downtown department stores slipped at least 10 percent annually, and retailers reacted by concentrating their investments in their largely successful suburban stores.[107] Hutzler's George Bernstein says, "We were eating our own business with the suburban stores." In 1975, the mayor's office released a downtown feasibility study stating that two department stores were likely to close within the next five years. The city tried to implement a $210 million face-lift for the Howard and Lexington shopping district called the Lexington Center. The project included a roof over Lexington Street, along with people movers and multiple parking garages, but the plan's completion was "a ways down the road." Mayor Schaefer stressed that "some of these stores can't afford to hold on for two to three years." The first store to pull up its stakes was Hochschild's.

On January 21, 1977, Hochschild, Kohn announced that it would cease operations at its downtown store the following July. The antiquated store spread throughout eight adjoining buildings, but at least half of its space was unused. Kohn family member Liz Moser remembers the downtown Hochschild's as "a terrible mess, but it all held together." Vice-president and

Shoppers wait outside the closed downtown Hochschild, Kohn store in 1978. *Special Collections, University of Maryland Libraries.*

Hochschild, Kohn opened a mostly apparel store at the Harford Mall in October 1977. After closing its downtown store in July 1977, Hochschild's opened smaller stores that were less costly to operate. The Harford Mall Hochschild's operated as a Hutzler's from 1984 to 1987. *Collection of the author.*

Secretary Dick Wyman says, "The space was poorly configured. It was a difficult piece of property, especially after we had installed the escalators." Upon the store's closure, one letter to the *Baltimore Sun* read, "To me, the heart of the Howard and Lexington street intersection, abuzz with heavy traffic, holiday decorations, Salvation Army music and happy chatter of Christmastime won't be there this winter."[108] Hochschild, Kohn had been in a retrenchment plan for many years and decided that its future was in Baltimore's northern suburbs. "Hochschild's put all their marbles into trying to find a new location near Towson," says former advertising employee Louise White. "They had outgrown Belvedere, and they hoped a new store would be their salvation." Hochschild's wanted to experience the same success that Hutzler's Towson enjoyed. Unfortunately, "everything that worked at Hutzler's didn't work at Hochschild's," says White. Hochschild's settled for three small stores at the Harford Mall, North Plaza Mall and Kenilworth Bazaar in Towson. All three stores, or "twigs," were intended to replace volume loss created by the downtown store's closing. "Kenilworth didn't do the business that they needed to do," says employee Pat Leibowitz, nor did any of the three stores ever achieve anticipated sales figures. As the company struggled with "constantly thinking in terms of what Hochschild's is, not what it should be,"[109] Hochschild, Kohn decided that its future was in trading down.

Howard Street's troubles continued as Stewart's announced its downtown store's closure on January 3, 1979. The announcement was not a total surprise to the retail community. The previous summer, Stewart's had moved its executive offices to the Reisterstown Road Plaza store and had made a significantly smaller order of spring merchandise.[110] Stewart's Howard Street store had been losing money for the past ten years, and its parent, Associated Dry Goods, refused to continue the store's losses, citing "the erosion of sales as sizeable." Additionally, at least $2 million was needed just to bring the building up to modern standards. The downtown Stewart's still used the Lamson tube system. Buyer Don Alexander recalls, "One [tube] system ran to the basement for change while the other system went to the eighth floor for orders and credit. It ran until the day the store closed. It was an antiquated system, but there was no reason to change it."

Alexander felt that the store's closing was inevitable: "All of the Stewart's stores were failing badly." But he recalls a certain event when he knew the store's future was in doubt:

Crowds descend on the downtown Stewart's store for its final liquidation sale in January 1979. *Special Collections, University of Maryland Libraries.*

Workers begin to dismantle the unsold fixtures at the downtown Stewart's in January 1979. *Special Collections, University of Maryland Libraries.*

*I remember being at a buying meeting where I raised my hand and asked,
"When will Stewart's start selling by UPC code?" I was told that that
was not going to happen. I turned to my boss and said, "We're going out
of business." Also, as an expense-cutting measure, the company decided to
do away with assistant managers.*

Thousands jammed the aisles of Stewart's for its Once-in-a-Lifetime Sale
at the Howard Street store. The once-quiet store that had served a former
carriage-trade customer base was so crowded with bargain hunters that
the fire department had to limit traffic into the building even as throngs
of shoppers overtaxed the store's escalator system. Police had trouble
controlling the crowds that were estimated to be about twelve thousand
people for the sale's opening day. Buyer Susan Newmsman recalls the day
of the sale:

*I remember the doors opening for the closing sale and seeing people pouring
up the escalator. I was wondering, "Why couldn't this have happened
before?" We* [the employees] *spent most of our time just picking stuff
off of the floor. It was a very emotional time. I kept thinking, "How could
they leave this beautiful building empty?"*

Although the downtown store was shuttered, Stewart's remained
committed to its five suburban stores. "It is our intention to be more
aggressive in the Baltimore market," promised store president Edward M.
Condon.[111] Former Stewart's president Leonard Levey says, "The store was
having a difficult time since the city was changing. Stewart's was chugging
along, but it needed a push. We saw that there was an opening if we paid a
more sophisticated attention to assortments." Levey believes that Stewart's
had an advantage over Hutzler's: "Hutzler's customers were real old-timers,
and we also had some of them. Hutzler's was still trying to be everything
to everybody, and the newcomers hadn't entered the market yet." Stewart's
focused a lot of energy on its Timonium store. "We used Timonium as our
experimental store," continues Levey. "We added additional assortments,
and it worked very well."

Unfortunately, Stewart's efforts to survive and thrive in the suburbs were
thwarted as out-of-town merchants prepared to enter the Baltimore market.
These retailers challenged all of Baltimore's traditional department stores.
Bamberger's, a division of R.H. Macy from Newark, New Jersey, was an
aggressive retailer that saw an opening. The company noticed "a failure by

A closed entrance of Stewart's store on Lexington Street. *Collection of the author.*

Stewart's Timonium store was connected to a small shopping mall that housed such locations as Hamburgers men's store, Martin's Shoes, Walden Books and the Timonium Cheese Shop. The Timonium Mall was developed by Stewart's and opened on February 1, 1971. On February 26, 1983, it was the final Stewart's location to close its doors. *Courtesy of the Baltimore County Public Library Legacy Web.*

existing Baltimore chains to plan properly for an upscale market." In 1979, Bamberger's announced it would build a location at the White Marsh Mall in Baltimore's northern suburbs. Upon its initial announcement of entering the Baltimore market, Bamberger's began to actively recruit buyers from Hutzler's and Stewart's. Woodward & Lothrop would also join Bamberger's as an anchor store. "Woodward & Lothrop was the Hutzler's of Washington, but it still didn't have the reputation," says Huztler's executive Dan Sachs. Garfinckels and Saks Fifth Avenue also expressed interest in the Baltimore market. In 1981, rumors circulated that Bloomingdale's might build a new department store on Pratt Street in the growing Inner Harbor area.

When Bamberger's arrived in 1981, Hutzler's met the store head-on at White Marsh. Customers flocked to the area's largest mall, but they were

Shoppers cross Howard Street in front of the downtown Baltimore Hecht's store in the early 1980s. *Special Collections, University of Maryland Libraries.*

Hutzler's opened a small location on Lombard Street, near the Inner Harbor, on March 3, 1980. The ready-to-wear only store sold "all cottons and wovens, no doubleknits." *Collection of the author.*

interested primarily in Bamberger's and Woodward & Lothrop. Hutzler's first suburban store in over sixteen years was quiet. But it was even quieter at Stewart's five branch locations, where the company's hope for the future turned into a constant downward spiral.

In 1981, Stewart's parent company, Associated Dry Goods, referred to Stewart's as a "trouble spot." Its customer base was aging along with its stores. The company opted not to expand into the wave of Baltimore's new shopping malls because it "hadn't yet heard of a shopping center constructed far enough away from our existing stores." Former president Levey says, "Associated Dry Goods made the decision to change the direction of the stores." On November 3, 1982, ADG announced the closure of the Stewart's stores in Baltimore. They were replaced with the company's Caldor discount stores. It was the end of an era for Baltimore's "most popular outsider." The *Baltimore Sun* stated:

Done in finally by the energy and resources of immigrant stores from New Jersey and Washington, and in the end only a collection of five suburban outlets without a center, Stewart's was once the monarch of department stores here. In its white Victorian palace on Howard Street, it was polish and chauffeurs and white gloves. It was buyers shuttling off to New York and Europe. It was, according to the boast, one of the largest department stores south of the Mason-Dixon line. [112]

Clearance sales began in early January 1983. Stewart's closure devastated Manager Edwina Smith. "Many people were very sad about its closing, but most people were just looking for good buys. It was hard to believe that the store was closing," says Smith. A number of employees were furious that the headquarters had changed this beloved department store into a discount store. "They had to fill it with something," says buyer Don Alexander. Buyer Susan Nehmsmann laments, "Turning Stewart's into Caldor was like putting a knife in my heart." She continues, "A lot of people thought that Hutzler's was the only store." Hutzler's was the high-profile prestige store in Baltimore, but thousands of Baltimoreans shopped at Stewart's, especially at its popular York Road store.

Hutzler's, the doyenne of Howard Street, survived the closing of Hochschild's and Stewart's, but rumors swirled about an impending closure. Hutzler family member George Bernstein says, "Downtown was a huge piece of property, and it was expensive to operate. The store was way beyond its life." Those Baltimoreans who still traveled downtown noticed that Hutzler's was losing its upscale status on Howard Street and looking more like a clearance outlet. It still continued many of its traditions, but those traditions were outdated and costly. The *Baltimore Sun* stated:

It still has elevator operators, friendly operators who greet passengers by their first names. It still uses silverware in the restaurant, heavy silverware with the company initials on it. And the coffee comes with cream, real cream. This was a store where on Thanksgiving Eve proud natives took out-of-towners to see the decorations. These were the stores where it felt like Christmas. Hutzler's [downtown] has its holiday decorations up but the busy stores will be the ones in the shopping malls. [113]

Hutzler's had limited cash to boost its business and improve its buildings. Baltimore's banks were generous in extending credit to keep the business viable, but that practice couldn't last forever. David Hutzler admits, "Hutzler's never made a lot of money." George Bernstein agrees, "It was obvious that we didn't make any money. We didn't make any appreciable amount of profit, and we were unable to reasonably expand." Hutzler's 1980 expansion was a poorly located, undersized store near Baltimore's Inner Harbor. City leaders wondered if the Inner Harbor store was meant to replace the Howard Street store. Downtown Baltimore's department store leadership cited shoplifting, poor police protection, streetside grime, a shortage of accessible inexpensive parking and traffic congestion as reasons for the store's troubles.[114]

W. Austin Kenly became the president and chief executive officer of Hutzler's on December 13, 1977. A former executive from Black & Decker, Kenly was the first non–family member to lead the organization. He was expected to improve the company's finances, and Kenly's work was challenging from the start. He wanted Hutzler's to continue "to merit its reputation as the outstanding department store chain in the Baltimore area," but he struggled with aging stores, declining market share and family infighting. Kenly had no retail experience, and he brought in a regime that drew very mixed reviews. Barbara Bailey came from I. Magnin & Co. and joined Hutzler's as its executive vice-president of sales promotion. The traditional Hutzler employee remained on the job for years, possibly decades. Longtime employees viewed Bailey as an outsider who didn't understand Baltimore. One manager called her a "dud." Another dedicated employee complained that Bailey's logo and color choices made Hutzler's feel less prestigious. But buyer Sandy Schmidt says, "Barbara Bailey tried to connect the store to Baltimore. She did her homework." The mix of new staff and longtime employees was tense and unhealthy. Even Sue Sachs, who loved her job and says, "It was like heaven!" felt it was time to leave. "I was so happy to get out. I didn't like the people that I was working for, and the writing was on the wall."

George Bernstein was the last Hutzler family member involved in the management of the business, and he left the store in 1982. Citing reasons why Hutzler's struggled, Bernstein says:

> *Hutzler's overbuilt their stores for the amount of volume that they were going to do. They also stocked their stores with expensive merchandise that they had to mark down in price and lost money. None of the stores ever reached its sales potential. Even when we made a profit, it was paltry. Hutzler's went the way of every other store in the world. Our story wasn't much different than other stores, except that we were nicer people.*

A quiet view of the downtown Hecht's store in the early 1980s, prior to its renovation and downsizing. *Special Collections, University of Maryland Libraries.*

Hecht's shrank and modernized its huge downtown store at Howard and Lexington Streets. The seven-month renovation included the demolition of every wall and every floor of the fifty-five-year-old store. In addition, locations at the lucrative Security Square Mall and the former Korvettes store in the Harford Mall were opened. A new flagship store was built in Towson on land owned by Hutzler's. Hecht's freestanding Towson store was destined to become part of the planned Towsontowne Centre shopping complex. Hutzler family member George Bernstein says, "We owned all of this property from our Towson store all of the way to Goucher, and there was this opportunity for us to join this monstrous thing [Towsontowne Centre]. We thought that we were going to get rich off of the [ground] rent." Hecht's also blanketed the Baltimore area with credit promotions and upgraded and expanded its merchandise offerings. By the time Bamberger's arrived in Baltimore in 1981, Hecht's was ready and waiting for it. The store actually increased its market share in spite of Bamberger's newness and popularity.

In 1981, Hutzler's employed 2,029 employees and had sales of $65 million, of which $25 million came from the Towson store. However, in 1972, annual sales were $72 million. The Hutzler family interests controlled virtually all stock, and family members filled four of the eight board of director positions. As Bamberger's entered Baltimore and Hecht's strengthened its stores, Hutzler's was unprepared to fight for its market share. "We stood on our little perch, as snotty as hell, and didn't want to deal with those other people," says George Bernstein. "We wanted to be on top of the retailing pyramid and didn't want to adjust [the business]." Bernstein sees this as a fatal mistake but also feels that the store was too troubled for a turnaround. By the end of 1982, financial conditions prompted Hutzler's to investigate liquidation proceedings or search for a potential suitor. The company found Angelo Arena. Arena came to Baltimore with impressive credentials and brought an infusion of new capital to the longtime family business. Arena brought Edward Blair as a substantial investor, and both received seats on the store's board of directors. Arena was appointed president and chief executive officer on May 16, 1983. With a substantial ownership stake in the company, Arena had grand plans for Hutzler's and was eager to implement them.

Arena planned to change the structure of Hutzler's. In August 1984, Hutzler's purchased four of the largest Hochschild, Kohn stores in the Baltimore market from their parent company, Supermarkets General. This move made Hutzler's the largest department store in Baltimore in terms of square footage, and Arena believed it would increase its market share. The four stores involved in the acquisition were Harford Mall, Harundale Mall, Eastpoint Mall and Security Square Mall, the prize of the purchase. The purchase was praised and also questioned by retail analysts. Many of the new locations were within a couple miles of existing Hutzler's stores. Two months later, Arena purchased the high-end specialty women's clothier Sara Fredericks. It was part of Hutzler's commitment to "deemphasize lower promotional price lines and place more emphasis on fashionable upscale lines."[115] The purchase was controversial. Buyer Pat Leibowitz remembers meeting with a merchandising representative and telling him that Angelo Arena was good and that the company was proud of Hutzler's new direction: "He [the rep] looked at me and said, 'He [Arena] destroyed all of the other stores, and he'll destroy Hutzler's too.'"

Hutzler's longtime competitor, Hochschild's, practically transformed into a discount operation that turned only modest profits.[116] In December 1982, the vacant Hochschild, Kohn building at Howard and Lexington Streets began its conversion into the Atrium, a mixed-use building intended

The Hochschild, Kohn store at York Road and Belvedere Avenue shortly before the marginally profitable store closed in January 1984. *Special Collections, University of Maryland Libraries.*

to be the centerpiece of Market Center, Baltimore's new Howard Street district. California developer David Murdock planned the $250 million complex that included Maryland's largest and tallest office buildings. On February 17, 1983, a ten-alarm fire roared through the Hochschild building. It was damaged beyond repair and was demolished quickly. In May 1983, Hutzler's announced a partnership plan with the city to build a new store on the site of the former Hochschild's. It meant the closure of its outdated, shabby yet iconic Howard Street store. Arena invested $6 million of Hutzler's funds to build the new dream store. It was scheduled to open in early 1985.

Many people questioned Hutzler's ability to bring high-end shoppers back downtown. The area had changed, along with its demographics and clientele. Even Brager-Gutman, Baltimore's value-oriented department store, called it quits two days after Christmas 1984. On December 26,

On February 17, 1983, a ten-alarm fire destroyed the vacant Hochschild, Kohn structure. At the time of the fire, the building was being prepared for renovation. The historic structure was unable to be saved, and its remains were quickly cleared. *Special Collections, University of Maryland Libraries*.

180 employees were presented with a terse note detailing the final liquidation sale scheduled to start the following day at the Lexington Street store, as well as at a branch on Liberty Road in Woodmoor. Many workers were astonished by owner Harry Weinberg's final decision. Other Brager-Gutman executives were not surprised by the closure. One manager said, "The only indication that we've had is that business has been very bad for a number of years. I'm losing my job, but I'd have closed the store two years ago."[117] The closing of Brager-Gutman's did not shock former family executive Henry Gutman. "Gutman's was minimally profitable, and not even every year," says Gutman. The building did not lay vacant for a long period. Epstein's, a value retailer from Highlandtown, Gay Street and surrounding areas, moved into the former Gutman's store. Founded in 1926, Epstein's catered to the same demographic as Brager-Gutman's. However, by January 1991, "crimped consumer spending and a recessive economy" forced the closure of all seven remaining Epstein's stores, including its flagship location on Lexington Street.[118]

Crowds gather at the grand opening of Hutzler's new Palace store on April 1, 1985. Hutzler's vacated its Art Deco building and consolidated all business into this new flagship. The store was a financial disaster from day one and choked the company's finances. *Collection of the author.*

On April 1, 1985, Hutzler's downtown Palace opened, replacing the Art Deco emporium that Baltimore grew up with and ushering in a new era of downtown retailing. Angelo Arena envisioned hordes of downtown workers and potential lunchtime shoppers coming to the new store. Industry experts felt the money would have been better spent fixing up the chain's aging suburban locations.[119] Hutzler's Palace store carried merchandise by designers such as Gucci, Fendi and Armani. Employees questioned the store's purpose since Baltimore's remaining downtown customers were typically low income. The crime rate at Howard and Lexington Streets was high, and the area was under massive long-term construction as the Light Rail system was installed. "Why would you open a store with Armani clothing in the middle of a ghetto?" asks employee Hannah Mazo. Employee Pat Leibowitz questions, "What was the purpose of that store [Hutzler's Palace]? For the goods to be stolen?" Stories circulated about racks of designer clothing being literally rolled out the store's front doors. The store was a financial disaster from the day it opened.

By August, the company was struggling with high inventory levels and severe cash flow problems. Hutzler's, once the darling of fashion wholesalers and financial institutions, found itself fighting to fill its eleven stores with merchandise and get lines of credit. Many loyal employees saw the writing on the wall and resigned. Buyer Sue Gaston Sachs left the company she once loved and rarely returned for visits. "The one thing that I feel bad about is that I think I only went back in Hutzler's twice after I left [in 1985]. I can remember going back a year later after the buying offices moved from downtown to Towson. It was depressing, and you could see the strain on the store," says Sachs. Former executive Peter Rosenwald worked, at one time or another, for Hecht's, Hochschild's, Stewart's and Hutzler's. He jokes that he "has the distinction of closing all four stores." Rosenwald left Hutzler's just before the palace store opened. "I left because I didn't want to wait around for it to fail," explains Rosenwald. By January 1986, just nine months after the opening of the downtown palace store and the company's attempt to remake Hutzler's into Baltimore's high-fashion retail leader, Hutzler's made an about-face and concentrated on traditional moderately priced merchandise. The strategy was too little too late. On June 13, 1987, Hutzler's began a Sale on Everything at its Westview, Harford and Salisbury stores. The company advertised, "History is being made with this sale…A sale that you'll talk about for years!" Over the next two years, Hutzler's painfully closed store after store and entered into a joint partnership with liquidator Jerome Schottenstein.

Hecht's dominated the retail market through the 1980s, taking advantage of Hutzler's struggles, aggressively tackling Bamberger's (later Macy's) youthful customer base and opening new stores. After several renovation attempts, Hecht's announced the closure of its longtime Northwood and Reisterstown Road Plaza stores in January 1986. Northwood, Hecht's first Baltimore branch store and the site of the famous restaurant sit-in demonstrations, was once the company's most profitable location. By 1983, it was a money loser in a declining neighborhood. Hecht's saw its future in the new mega shopping centers like Owings Mills and Marley Station in Glen Burnie. Employee Edwina Smith remembers being told that "Owings Mills was the up-and-coming shopping center and that it was going to do very well. It did for a couple of years." The Owings Mills store replaced the Plaza location, despite renovations. Smith recalls, "We always wondered why they would redo the store and then close it." August 1986 saw the closure of the final four Hochschild, Kohn stores. Once a major force, Hochschild's had become an afterthought in Baltimore's retail market. Its Eastpoint Mall location quickly transitioned into a closeout retailer called Hochschild's Value City. The same format was later implemented at Hutzler's former Westview Mall store.

Downtown Baltimore suffered a two-punch knockout in the fall of 1988. Angelo Arena notified the landlord of the Hutzler's palace store, Murdock Development Co., and the city, to whom it owed $2 million for an Urban Development Action Grant, that the downtown store would close after the Christmas 1988 selling season. This was followed by Hecht's similar closure announcement on October 19, 1988. The company said it had been "unable to achieve acceptable productivity standards for many years" at its downtown location.[120] This statement baffled columnist Jacques Kelly. "The downtown Hecht's was [usually] mobbed with people until the day it closed," says Kelly. Hecht's store at Howard and Lexington Streets was "a victim of changing times and the city's unsuccessful efforts to revitalize a once-vibrant downtown corridor."[121] It closed its doors on January 28, 1989.

Hutzler's palace store finally closed in February 1989 after spending its last months as a clearance center. Employee Hannah Mazo worked for the company throughout its final months. She blames Hutzler's problems on one bad decision after another. She remembers one particular instance that became company legend:

> One of our buyers went out and bought a huge amount of Fostoria glassware. There were just carloads of it, and it was ugly as sin. It could fill a number of railroad cars, and there was no room for it in the stores. Everywhere in the stores, there was Fostoria glass, even in the men's room. They finally began to mark it down over and over until it was almost a penny apiece, but there was still a ton of it left. Finally, one executive decided to take care of the problem. We left a tractor trailer unlocked at the Westview loading dock and filled it with old escalator parts and the remaining Fostoria glassware. The next day, all of the escalator parts were gone but the Fostoria glass was still there!

After terminating pension plans, health insurance plans and store leases, and unable to obtain credit for merchandise, Hutzler's began to wind down its entire business in mid-1989. Even Hutzler's downtown palace store, the 1985 long-suffering prototype for a reenergized business, finally ended its run on February 18, 1989. The company closed store after store as it searched for some way to keep the business as an ongoing concern. Former employee Louise White recalls Albert J. Hutzler III telling her, "The sad thing is that we have long been gone from the store but [unfortunately] our name is still on the building." As the company's only remaining member of the personnel department, Hannah Mazo notified employees, one person at a time, that they were losing their jobs. Mazo says:

> *It was very difficult* [informing people] *because these people had given twenty, thirty and forty years of service. It was devastating. They just didn't have any other plans. One woman cried so hysterically that I had to pick her up off the floor. Some people were very surprised at the closure, but I wanted to say, "Look what's happening! There's no merchandise!"*

Hutzler's Towson store, the company's final location, began its liquidation sale in October 1989. Mazo says, "The liquidators were brisk, demeaning and condescending. They had no respect for the institution that they were

The once-popular Hutzler's in Towson prior to its closing in January 1990. *Courtesy of the Baltimore County Public Library Legacy Web.*

putting down." Buyer Sandy Schmidt remained until the end and says, "We tried to keep it Hutzler's. Those of us who stayed did so because we lived here and we were like loyal family members." Regarding the store's final liquidation, Mazo remembers, "I thought we were too big to fail. We were too nice to fail." On October 24, 1989, three board members, including Angelo Arena, met briefly and approved the distribution of all remaining assets to the store's creditors. After 132 years and decades of financial and institutional struggles, Hutzler's never filed for bankruptcy. On January 28, 1990, the store that was too big and too nice to fail failed. David A. Hutzler says, "Hutzler's demise started the day Luskin's opened. We had no way to fight them. Competition is good until you're the one getting beaten down."

Baltimore's department store market rested in the hands of Hecht's, Macy's and Woodward & Lothrop. The latter, known as Woodies, was an independent Washington-based retailer with area locations in White Marsh, Columbia and Annapolis. It faced its own demise in August 1995. With financial and managerial support from its parent company, the May Department Stores Company, Hecht's continued to expand throughout the region as it gobbled up retailers such as Richmond-based Thalhimers and Philadelphia's John Wanamaker and Strawbridge and Clothier stores.

Hecht's was a powerhouse department store with eighty-one stores located from Philadelphia to Wilmington, North Carolina, to Nashville, Tennessee. It employed five thousand workers and made over $2.3 billion in annual sales. But by the early 2000s, its parent company had grown complacent. The stores were lackluster and overstocked with merchandise. Hecht's customers were trained to shop at its weekly promotional sales that included endless coupon savings. It was a place for necessities rather than luxuries. One retail analyst said, "There was nothing special, no excitement in the company. There was no special reason to go to the Hecht Company."

On July 28, 2005, Federated Department Stores announced its $10.4 billion purchase of the May Department Stores Company. As expected, Federated promised upgraded merchandise and the discontinuation of May's regional nameplates. Upon this announcement, the *Baltimore Sun* reported, "Poor Hecht's. The retail world changed, but Hecht's didn't. It lumbered on like a sleeping giant as Nordstrom arrived to feed a booming demand for luxury items on the one end and nimbler, better-priced outlets like Wal-Mart, Target, and Kohl's served the other end."[122]

A 1953 busy view of Lexington Street, looking west from Liberty Street to Howard Street. Julius Gutman's, the May Co. and Hochschild, Kohn are clearly visible in the photograph. *Special Collections, University of Maryland Libraries.*

The same view fifty-seven years later in 2010. *Photograph by the author.*

On September 9, 2006, the Hecht name disappeared and was replaced by the name Macy's, Federated's signature business. The change marked the end of a storied name in Baltimore's retail history. In 2006, *Style* magazine wrote, "If the other chains were the elegant doyennes of Baltimore shopping, Hecht's was the plucky working-class shopgirl—relying on the methods pioneered by Moses Hecht, pulling herself up by her bootstraps and constantly reinventing herself. If for nothing else, Hecht's is worthy of remembering, and worthy of missing."[123]

Message Book

In February 1969, I had to join the military. I was sad to leave Hutzler's, and the staff had a very sweet and somber going-away party. I still have the pictures and the cards, which all contained cash. At that time, the Hutzler policy was that if you had to enter the military, you would still receive a monthly check for the amount between the Hutzler's salary and the military salary. And so for the next few years, my wife received that check, which decreased as my military salary increased. But it was still over $100. I retained my 20 percent employee discount, received copies of the *Tips and Taps* magazine and a $100 holiday gift each December. Believe me, we really needed the money, but I knew that my position, or one equal, was waiting for me when I was discharged. *This* is what made Hutzler's so great.
—Jay W.

All of the stores were so close, and when you went downtown, you went to all four stores—except Stewart's. Stewart's was known as a "fuddy-duddy" store and was too old-fashioned. I so loved Hecht's and went there all of the time. One time, Hecht's had a Christmas display window that centered on King Kong. It was really fun, but the customers didn't like it. Their designers were very risqué and were just expressing themselves. I guess things were changing too fast. I was so sad when Hecht's closed. Now all we have is Macy's.
—Elaine C.

I miss all of the grand department stores that were in downtown: Hutzler's, Hecht's, etc. Downtown will never be the same without those "grand ladies." Being African American and growing up in Maryland, I had to endure not being able to shop in Hutzler's. (It was OK if we worked there.) I remember traveling by streetcar downtown and being able to only shop at select stores such as Brager-Gutman's. As a child, this reality was a puzzle.
—BCD

As a kid, I lived within a few blocks of Hochschild's Belvedere, yet we always went to Hutzler's Towson store. My brother was engaged to a girl who worked in the jewelry department, and I dated her friend. I can still remember buying the "alligator" shirts at Hutzler's that we all wore at Towson High. (No one called them "Lacoste" in those days.) My family still laughs about the time when I was sixteen and I tried to order rum cake in Hutzler's Valley View Room. The waitress refused to serve it to me because I wasn't twenty-one yet! It was a different world then.
—Stu

I loved Hutzler's like no other store. One of the true joys and highlights of my youth was the weekly trip with my mother to Hutzler's. I even loved the parking garage with that fabulously cozy little waiting room. There was an attendant stationed outside of the entrance to the garage on Eutaw Street, and if the garage was filled, he waved you by. I was almost ill at the thought that we'd have to park at Hochschild's! What a store. What a time.
—Ann

My grandmother and my sister loved nothing more than going downtown. You would have thought that they had gone to the moon and back. In reality, they had only jumped on the #11 bus that went down Charles Street. I still think that the closest that I have ever been to heaven was at Hutzler's downtown, eating Saratoga chips and drinking a Shirley Temple. The escalators were like stairs to heaven.
—Lacey C.

I have so many memories of Hutzler's in Towson. I have wonderful memories of running around the toy department while my mother shopped. We had many wonderful meals in the Valley View Room. The food was always so good there, and my grandmother loved to buy things from the bakery. One funny memory—although it was not very funny at the time—was when I had to entertain my new two-year-old brother while my mother shopped. For forty-five minutes, I took my brother up and down the escalator. Every time I tried to get off, he would scream bloody murder. I should have gotten a lot of allowance money for that.

One time, my grandparents took us down to the downtown Hutzler's and we had lunch. It was like being on another planet. When I got my driver's license, I became my grandmother's shuttle service to Hutzler's. When I heard about the store closing, it broke my heart. Although I had gone to the Hutzler's at the Harford Mall a few times in later years, it was the Towson store that stole my heart and was like a family member to me.

There was something different and magical about Hutzler's. Yes, we sometimes shopped at Stewart's, Hecht's and Hochschild's, but they always paled in comparison.
—Jennifer W.

I have so many memories of growing up in Baltimore in the 1960s and '70s when the "Big Four" department stores flourished. I have many memories of Hutzler's, where my brother-in-law worked in the display department for over twenty years. I remember the balcony entrance from Saratoga Street and how you had to cross Clay Street to go from the Art Deco building to the original palace building. (You felt like you were in a tunnel of sorts.) My last visit to the store was in October 1985, at the new palace location, where I recall buying a shirt. I gained a greater appreciation of how special Hutzler's was as the premier Baltimore department store and the great pride employees took in their work and connection to the store. I witnessed this firsthand.
—Kenneth C.

My father worked for thirty-six years at the Baltimore Post Office and also worked part time during a couple of holiday seasons at Hutzler's downtown. I worked at the Howard Street store a few evenings a week when I was in high school on the fifth-floor housewares wrapping desk, where I prepared packages to be delivered by truck. We loved hopping on a streetcar and shopping at those downtown stores. You can't find that kind of atmosphere today.

My dad was waiting for a bus on his way to work on a cold February morning in 1983 and saw smoke coming from the Hochschild's building. He pulled the firebox that sent fire engines to what would become a six-alarm fire that destroyed the building.
—Tom C.

I remember the big Santa on top of the Westview Hutzler's and the restaurant. I used to order the ice cream for dessert. They used to decorate it like a clown: sugar cone for a hat, candies for a face and whipped cream for a ruffled collar. It was quite magical when you were a kid. If there is any doubt that I am a sucker for Baltimore nostalgia, just let me tell you that I keep my grandmother's old Charge-a-Plate in my purse for good luck.
—Margaret

I am eighty-three years old. My grandmother found a job as the chief cook for Mrs. Hutzler. She came from Germany and used to work as a cook over there. My grandmother used to go to Lexington Market to a butcher and came to find out that it was a man that was on the same boat that she traveled from Germany. For years, my grandmother would always get Mrs. Hutzler's meat from the same butcher, as she always liked the kind and cut of meat he always gave her.

My mom used to take me when I was a little girl on Saturdays to Lexington Market and then to Hutzler's, where we used to shop and eat lunch. The store was just beautiful. My mom used to buy there all the time, and as I got older, I also shopped there.
PS: The butcher, as time went on, became my grandfather.
—Ruth H.

There was an eccentric old rich lady who owned a lot of property in Lutherville that shoplifted at the Hutzler's in Towson. Whatever she stole or skipped out on in the dining room was promptly recorded by the nearby sales clerk or waitress. This information was turned into management, and her accountant got a bill. She was one of the store's best customers.
—Bob S.

I would go to O'Neill's because it was my mother's tradition. It was the only store where you could walk up to a window and look at something in broad daylight. In the early 1920s, my mother and her sister attended Girls' Latin School. One day, the school received a call from O'Neill's asking for them to "send the girls down to O'Neill's to try on some new dresses." The idea of pulling two girls out of school to try on new merchandise was just bizarre!
—Louise

I worked at the Hub in the late '40s. It was nothing spectacular, but it was very neat in appearance. The Hub had plenty of rodents, big rats. The damn

things would crawl into the cabinets and die. You could always tell where the rats were because of the odor. I was the low man on the totem pole, so it was my job to take care of it. Rats are just a fact of life in downtown Baltimore.
—J.D.

Joel Gutman & Co. was a wonderful store in its prime. The store was killed when the [Lexington] Market expanded. There were stalls all up and down Eutaw Street. If you had to work at night, you had to fight the rats. They would be running all over the place. The market was alive with rats. It was a feast for rats, and they lived very high on that.

Gypsies would always stop into the store whenever they were traveling through Baltimore. You could tell that they were gypsies by the way they dressed and the way they talked. Whenever the gypsies came into the store, a half a dozen of us were assigned to watch them. They could easily throw you off enough and always ended up stealing something.

It was very sad when we closed [in June 1929]. People came from all over to say goodbye. I always thought, "Why didn't you come here and shop when you could?"
—Arthur Gutman, grandnephew and employee, Joel Gutman & Co., 1928–29

You went to Hutzler's when you wanted to get something real good. It was just a nice, clean, well-kept store. The big shots in town went to the Colonial Restaurant [at Hutzler's]. I used to fake that I was a waiter just to get in. I used to think that Hutzler's was the best store in town, but I got into a debate on that with Walter Sondheim at Hochschild, Kohn. Hochschild's was a little different. It was rough and ready. When you went into Hutzler's, you knew you were going into a palace. When you walked into Hochschild's, you walked into a house. Hochschild's was for common people like me.

I didn't think much of Stewart's. They were real outsiders. If you wanted to get the good stuff, you went to Hutzler's. If you wanted to get the ordinary stuff, you went to Hochschild, Kohn or the May Company.
—Governor William Donald Schaefer[124]

Tea for Two

Tearooms, restaurants and lunch counters played an important role in the success of many department stores. These restaurants were frequently considered the city's finest eating places.[125] Department store restaurants were rarely profitable but served as convenient, nice places to eat so that shoppers would not have to leave the store. Most importantly, these tearooms and restaurants played important social roles in a department store's business. Many young children learned etiquette at their lunch tables, and many women enjoyed special events such as fashion shows and fundraisers in these settings. A tearoom with good ambiance and signature dishes also drew new potential customers to the store.

All of Baltimore's department stores featured popular in-store restaurants. Hutzler's boasted the city's (arguably) most popular in-store restaurant. Its sixth floor housed the famous Colonial Restaurant, also known by most Baltimoreans as simply the "Tearoom," along with the Quixie. The Colonial was formal and elegant, while the Quixie served a limited menu and delivered quick service. Located downstairs was the Luncheonette, where diners stood patiently behind stools, waiting for one to become vacant. Its Annex housed the popular Fountain Shop, which catered to a younger clientele. Hochschild, Kohn featured its own fashionable tearoom, the Continental Room, found on the store's sixth floor. In 1953, May Company's Skyline Room was converted into the uniquely

A 1942 menu cover for Hutzler's Colonial Restaurant. The cover is designed by the popular cartoon artist of the *Baltimore Sun*, Richard Q. Yardley. *Collection of the author.*

designed Courtyard Restaurant on its eighth floor. Stewart's lesser-known Georgian Tea Room was located on the sixth floor and was eventually replaced by the Buffet restaurant on the store's main-floor balcony. Even the more value-oriented stores offered dining facilities. The Hub served lunch and dinner in its Chestnut Room restaurant along Fayette Street, and Brager-Gutman's offered a popular lunch counter and a downstairs dining room.

When Baltimore's department stores expanded to the area's suburbs, they brought along popular dining facilities. These restaurants played the same dining and social purposes as their downtown flagship counterparts. Hutzler's Valley View Room in Towson and its Maryland Gardens Restaurant in Westview were just as popular as Hochschild's Coffee Cup in Belvedere and Penguin Room in Eastpoint; Stewart's Terrace Room on York Road and Chesapeake Room at the Reisterstown Road Plaza; and Hecht Company's Rooftop Restaurant at Northwood and Silhouette Room at the Plaza.

As the downtown department stores deteriorated, so did the status and notoriety of the stores' restaurants. The once-prestigious dining rooms began to compete with newer, popular restaurants along Charles Street and the city's Inner Harbor. In the 1970s, *Baltimore Sun* food critic John Dorsey reviewed each of the department store tearooms on Howard Street and made some scathing comments and observations:

> *I must say I think of* [Hutzler's Colonial Restaurant] *as a woman's restaurant. One might also say a matron's restaurant. From the dusty blue wallpaper to the sprays of artificial flowers, the atmosphere consistently implies that the prime target of a department store is still the middle class married woman between the ages of 30 and 70. The crowd in* [Hochschild's Continental Room] *always looks the same—same motherly types (must get ample in description somewhere, ample shopping bags, ample hips, ample bosoms). Stewart's lunch room cannot be counted a success aside from its vaguely pleasant setting. The best of the food was indifferent, the worst was downright bad. Stewart's is a good department store, capable of a much better effort than this. It ought to be made.* [Hecht's Courtyard Restaurant] *is like one of those whiny maiden aunts who use their potential attributes to disadvantage whenever possible, and so end up lonely and bitter, blaming everybody else for their own faults. If it goes along as it does now, the Courtyard probably will close for sheer lack of business*

someday, and then everyone will say, "See, downtown is going to hell," when it won't be downtown but the Hecht Company that's to blame.[126]

Although Dorsey's comments are harsh, the reviews were indicative of the time period. They were a reflection of Howard Street's transformation from a bustling economic and entertainment epicenter to a tired and troubled urban wasteland. Dorsey's criticism does not acknowledge Baltimoreans' treasured memories of time spent shopping, socializing and dining.

The following are recipes that have been graciously donated by Baltimore's tearoom loyalists or interpreted through the painstaking research of these store's fragmented archives. Many of these recipes have been reprinted in various publications, but most have never been published in their correct, original form.

Hutzler's Crab Cakes

from the Colonial Restaurant

¾ Tablespoon dry mustard
⅛ teaspoon cayenne pepper
1 teaspoon Old Bay seasoning
2½ slices bread, crumbled
1 Tablespoon chopped fresh parsley
1 egg
3 Tablespoons mayonnaise
dash Tabasco sauce
1 pound backfin crabmeat

Mix all the dry ingredients. Add the slightly beaten egg, mayonnaise and Tabasco. Lastly, add the crabmeat and toss gently. Form into cakes. These can be fried or broiled. Makes seven three-ounce crab cakes.

Burgundy Beef on Parmesan Noodles

from Hutzler's Colonial Restaurant

1 medium onion
$^1\!/_2$ clove garlic
$^1\!/_2$ teaspoon oregano
$^1\!/_4$ teaspoon pepper
$^1\!/_2$ teaspoon salt
$2^2\!/_3$ cups brown gravy
2 pounds lean chuck (cut in one-inch cubes)
$^1\!/_4$ pound mushrooms (use canned if you like)
$^1\!/_3$ cup Burgundy wine
$^1\!/_2$ pound noodles
$2^2\!/_3$ cups chicken stock (use consommé if you have no stock)
1 teaspoon salt
MSG

Cook onions, garlic and seasonings in margarine or butter until onions are transparent. Add the brown gravy and the cubed beef. Cover and simmer until tender. Add the mushrooms and the wine. Serve over the noodles. Cook the noodles in the chicken stock with the salt and the MSG until noodles are tender. Do not drain. Add 1 Tablespoon each of butter, chopped fresh parsley and Parmesan cheese. Toss lightly.

Terrapin a la Maryland

from Hutzler's Colonial Restaurant

1 7-inch terrapin
$^1\!/_2$ stick butter
$2^2\!/_3$ cups chicken stock
$1^1\!/_3$ cups sherry
dash cayenne pepper

Heat the cooked terrapin meat (cut into half-inch pieces) with the butter. Add chicken stock, sherry and enough of the terrapin stock to make two quarts. Season to taste. You can make this in the kitchen, but it should be served from a chafing dish.

CHICKEN CHOW MEIN

from Hutzler's Valley View Room recipe files, with help from Amy Bernstein

1¾ pounds diced onions
1½ bunches diced celery
4 cups bean sprouts
12 ounces canned mushroom pieces
½ pound cooked shredded turkey
10 ounces cornstarch
10 cups chicken broth
4 Tablespoons soy sauce

In a large pot, cook onions and celery in a small amount of oil until tender. Add bean sprouts, mushrooms and turkey. (The chicken chow mein was actually made with shredded turkey, not chicken.) In a large bowl, blend cornstarch with two cups chicken broth. When smooth, add the rest of the chicken broth and soy sauce to bowl. Mix well and pour over meat and vegetables. Bring to a boil, stirring until sauce thickens. Reduce heat to low. Cover and simmer for ten to fifteen minutes. Serve over hot cooked rice and chow mein noodles. Serves ten.

SHRIMP SALAD

from Hutzler's Colonial Restaurant

2 cups large cooked, peeled and deveined shrimp, cut into pieces
2 cups medium cooked, peeled and deveined shrimp, cut into pieces
1 cup diced celery
1 teaspoon salt
¼ teaspoon pepper
¼ teaspoon Tabasco sauce
1 teaspoon Worcestershire sauce
3 Tablespoons catsup
1 Tablespoon prepared mustard
4 Tablespoons mayonnaise

Squeeze shrimp until they are dry. Mix together all remaining ingredients. Stir in shrimp and refrigerate. Makes one quart. Serve on toasted cheese bread or in avocado half with toasted English muffin.

Hutzler's Colonial Restaurant Cheese Bread

Courtesy of Hannah Mazo

¼ ounce yeast
3 Tablespoons warm water
3½ cups flour
pinch salt
2 teaspoons sugar
5⅓ ounces milk
4½ ounces grated sharp cheese
2 teaspoons margarine
2 teaspoons butter

Dissolve yeast in water. Knead all ingredients together while slowly adding flour. Cover and let mixture rise until it is double in size, about two hours. Place dough into greased 4x8 bread pan. Cover and let dough double in size. Bake for one hour at 300 degrees.

Cheese Straws

from Hutzler's downtown Bake Shop

8 ounces shredded sharp cheese
8 ounces margarine
2 cups flour
½ teaspoon red cayenne pepper
½ teaspoon paprika

Mix cheese with margarine and flour. Add red pepper and paprika. Mix together and chill. Cut into strips, five inches by half inch, after rolling dough. Bake at 400 degrees.

WELLESLEY FUDGE CAKE

from Hutzler's downtown Bake Shop

2 cups butter
6 cups sugar
12 eggs
1 quart buttermilk
¾ teaspoon baking soda
7½ cups cake flour
½ pound melted bitter chocoate
½ teaspoon vanilla

Cream butter and sugar; add eggs. Mix buttermilk and baking soda together. Then add alternately with flour to mix. Pour in melted chocolate and vanilla and mix thoroughly. This recipe makes two cakes. Bake at 350 degrees until thoroughly cooked, about twenty to twenty-five minutes. Ice cake while cake is still warm. You may add chopped pecans to batter and sprinkle on top of cake.

Wellesley Cake Icing

2½ ounces butter
1½ pounds bitter chocolate
3 pounds 4X powdered sugar
½ teaspoon vanilla
1½ cup Pet milk

Melt butter and chocolate. Mix together sugar, vanilla and milk. Add melting chocolate and butter. Mix together. Spread on cake while warm.

CREAM CHEESE CAKE

from Hutzler's downtown Bake Shop

Crust

¼ pound crumbled graham crackers
¼ pound margarine (room temperature)
¼ cup sugar

Filling

¾ pound cream cheese
¾ pound cottage cheese
3 eggs
4 Tablespoons table cream
¼ cup sugar
1 teaspoon lemon juice
½ teaspoon vanilla

Topping

½ pint sour cream
1 teaspoon sugar
drop of vanilla

Mix ingredients for the crust and press into ten-inch pie tin. Cream the cheese in your mixer and add the rest of the ingredients for your filling. Mix thoroughly. Bake at 350 degrees for forty to forty-five minutes. Let cool and spread with the topping. Bake another ten minutes. "This sounds a little fussy, but it is well worth the effort."

GOUCHER CAKE

from Hutzler's Valley View Room, Towson

1 cup butter or margarine
1¾ sugar
3¼ cups cake flour
5 teaspoons baking powder
½ teaspoon salt
1 cup milk
1 teaspoon almond extract
4 egg whites
chocolate icing (see below)
buttercream icing (see below)
¼ cup chopped almonds, for garnish

Preheat oven to 350 degrees. Cream butter and sugar. Sift the dry ingredients together and add them alternately with the milk and almond extract. Mix thoroughly. Beat egg whites until stiff but not dry and gently fold them into the batter. Pour batter into two greased and floured nine-inch cake pans. Bake at 350 degrees for about thirty-five minutes or until tester comes out clean. Cool completely before spreading chocolate icing between the layers and on the sides of the cake, and put buttercream icing on the top. Sprinkle with almonds.

Chocolate Icing

2 ounces bitter chocolate
⅓ cup butter
½ cup sugar
½ cup water
¾ cup confectioners' sugar
3 egg yolks
¼ teaspoon vanilla extract

Melt chocolate and add butter. Add sugar, water and confectioners' sugar. Cook until blended. Add the egg yolks and vanilla and cook for five minutes more. Split each cake layer in half and spread chocolate icing between the layers and on the sides but not the top.

Buttercream Icing

2 cups confectioners' sugar
2 Tablespoons butter, softened
½ teaspoon vanilla extract

Cream ingredients enough to make an icing. Spread on top of cake.

CHOCOLATE ICEBOX PUDDING

from Hutzler's Quixie, as interpreted by Ann Amernick

2½ cups whole milk
¾ cup sugar
1 envelope Knox gelatin
¼ cup water
3 ounces unsweetened chocolate (not bittersweet)
3 Tablespoons cornstarch
2 eggs
2 teaspoons vanilla extract

In a four-quart pot, add the milk and half of the ¾ cup sugar. Heat over medium heat, stirring to dissolve the sugar. While the milk is heating, in a small metal bowl, dissolve the gelatin in the cold water and let sit. When the gelatin has bloomed, dissolve it by placing the bowl that it is in in a larger bowl of very hot water and stir until liquid. Set aside. When the milk is hot, add the chocolate and stir to dissolve. Don't worry if the chocolate looks speckled and uncombined. Turn heat to low and continue to stir frequently. Combine the remaining ¾ cup of sugar with the cornstarch, and with a wire whisk, beat the eggs and combine with sugar/cornstarch mixture, beating until smooth and well combined. Temper the egg mix with the hot milk, a few ladles at a time, then add the egg mix to the pot and turn heat to medium high. At this point you'll beat continuously with the whisk until the mixture thickens and starts to "burp." Cook, stirring continuously, for two minutes over medium heat. Remove from heat, add the gelatin mix and vanilla and stir well to combine.

JUDY'S ICE CREAM CONE HAT

from Hutzler's Valley View Room, as remembered by Rebecca Hoffberger

1 scoop of vanilla ice cream
4-inch paper doily
1 sugar cone
2 raisins
1 shortbread cookie or vanilla wafer, shaped into a hooked nose
half of a maraschino cherry

Place ice cream scoop in small ice cream dish and top with paper doily. Place upside-down sugar cone on top of doily. Use two raisins for eyes, hooked cookie piece for nose and cherry half for mouth. Judy's appearance is based on the character from the famous puppet show Punch and Judy.

CUCUMBER DRESSING

from Hochschild's Continental Room

1 cucumber, grated
1 medium onion, grated
1 cup mayonnaise
⅓ cup vinegar
¼ cup water
½ teaspoon salt
½ teaspoon dry mustard
green vegetable coloring

Mix together all ingredients. Add green coloring to suit. Cover and refrigerate.

Chicken a la King

from Hochschild's Continental Room

3 Tablespoons butter
1 cup diced mushrooms
2 Tablespoons minced green pepper
4 Tablespoons flour
⅔ teaspoon salt
⅓ teaspoon celery salt
⅛ teaspoon cayenne pepper
1½ cups milk
1 cup chicken broth
3 cups cooked chicken, cut in 1½-inch pieces
1 Tablespoon minced parsley
1 Tablespoon diced pimento
2 egg yolks, slightly beaten
3 Tablespoons sherry

Melt the butter in a deep skillet. Add mushrooms and green pepper; cook until tender. Blend in flour, salt, celery salt and cayenne pepper. Slowly add milk and chicken broth, stirring constantly. Cook until sauce is thick and bubbly. Add chicken, parsley and pimento. Simmer for five minutes. While stirring the sauce, add the egg yolks and sherry. Simmer for another five minutes. Serve immediately over pastry shells.

"The Epicurean"

from Hecht's Courtyard Restaurant

1 large English muffin
2 one-ounce slices of ham
2 one-sounce slices of turkey
2 Tablespoons sliced canned mushrooms
cheese sauce (see below)
dried parsley

Lightly toast English muffin. Top one half of muffin with ham and the other half with turkey. Place one tablespoon of mushrooms on top of each muffin half. Cover each half with warm cheese sauce and sprinkle with dried parsley.

Cheese Sauce

⅓ cup milk
¼ cup mayonnaise
4 slices American cheese, coarsely chopped

Mix all ingredients in saucepan and heat to simmer, stirring occasionally.

Open-Face Tuna Melt

from Stewart's Buffet restaurant downtown; a popular sandwich during Lent

1 can tuna in water, drained
2 Tablespoons mayonnaise
1 teaspoon mustard
¼ teaspoon salt
⅛ teaspoon pepper
½ cup diced celery
1½ Tablespoon chopped onion
¾ teaspoon red wine vinegar
yellow cheese

Mix all ingredients together. Toast two slices of bread (white, wheat, rye or pumpernickel) lightly. Top each slice of bread with ½ of the amount of tuna salad. Top with a slice of yellow cheese. Place under broiler for one to two minutes, until cheese is bubbly.

CHERRY AND APPLE CAKE WITH VANILLA SAUCE

from Julius Gutman & Co.'s downstairs restaurant; only served during the store's famous Washington's Birthday Sale

6 green apples, peeled and thinly sliced
brown sugar and cinnamon
1 can cherry pie filling
1 cup flour
1 cup sugar
3 eggs
½ cup oil
2 teaspoons baking powder
vanilla sauce (see below)

Lightly grease a 9x13 pan. Cover bottom of pan with sliced apples. Sprinkle apples with brown sugar and cinnamon. Top with cherry pie filling. Mix together rest of ingredients and pour on top of filling. Sprinkle lightly with cinnamon. Bake in 350-degree oven for one hour or until toothpick comes out clean. Pour vanilla sauce over warm cake.

Vanilla Sauce

½ cup sugar
½ cup evaporated milk
½ teaspoon vanilla
¼ cup butter

Mix together sugar and milk and bring to a low boil. Cook for one minute. Whisk in vanilla and butter until well blended. Serve warm.

HORN & HORN MACARONI AND CHEESE

for a taste of Baltimore Street...

¼ pound macaroni
2 Tablespoons butter
1½ Tablespoons flour
¼ teaspoon salt
¼ teaspoon white pepper
1½ cups milk
½ pound cheddar cheese, cut into ¼-inch cubes
½ teaspoon Worcestershire sauce

Cook macaroni according to package directions. Melt butter over low heat. Whisk in flour, salt and pepper. Cook one to two minutes, or until a smooth mixture forms. Using a whisk, gradually blend in milk. Cook about five minutes, until mixture is thick and smooth. Remove from heat. In a large bowl, combine macaroni with the sauce, cheese and Worcestershire sauce. Pour into a greased 8x8 pan and bake at 375 degrees for twenty-five minutes, or until top begins to brown.

Notes

HUTZLER'S: WHERE BALTIMORE SHOPPED

1. *Baltimore Sun*, "Hutzler's: The Semi-Centennial Celebration Begins Tomorrow," March 1, 1908.
2. *Enterprising Emporiums* (Baltimore: Jewish Museum of Maryland, 2001), 12.
3. *Baltimore Sun*, "Hutzler Brothers' Magnificent New Store Opened for Inspection," September 18, 1888.
4. *Baltimore Sun*, Hutzler Brothers advertisement, February 3, 1886.
5. *Baltimore Sun*, Hutzler Brothers advertisement, Baltimore Sun, April 28, 1933.
6. *The Mercantile Career of the Hutzler Family* (Baltimore: Johns Hopkins University, 1939).
7. *Baltimore Sun*, "Joel Hutzler Dies at 84, Last of 3-Man Store Team," January 13, 1977.
8. *Baltimore Sun*, "Albert D. Hutzler, Merchant, Dead at 76," June 6, 1965.
9. *Baltimore Sun*, "Hutzler Project Begun at Towson: Ground Broken for Building of Suburban Center," June 23, 1950.
10. *Tips and Taps*, February 1953.
11. Samuel Feinberg, *What Makes Shopping Centers Tick* (New York: Fairchild Publications, 1960), 63.
12. Ibid., 64.
13. Louise White, interview with the author, March 25, 2012.
14. *New York Times*, "Carter Hawley Closing Held," October 26, 1990.

15. *Baltimore Sun*, "Albert D. Hutzler, Merchant, Dead at 76."

16. "A Pictoral History of the Hutzler Brothers Co.," Albert D. Hutzler Jr. presentation, 1968.

17. Gilbert Sandler, "We Had It All," *Jewish Times*, January 1997.

18. Jesse Glasgow, "Hutzler Calls Off Plan to Merge with Amfac," *Baltimore Sun*, August 27, 1972.

Better Try Hochschild, Kohn

19. "The Max Hochschild Story," Hochschild, Kohn & Co., June 1955.

20. *Baltimore Sun*, "New Department Store Contract Awarded by M. Hochschild & Co.," May 18, 1897.

21. *Baltimore Sun*, "Big Store Thrown Open," September 17, 1912.

22. Martin B. Kohn, "Hochschild, Kohn & Co.—A Personal Account," January 1979.

23. *Baltimore Sun*, "$2 Million Deal Said to Presage New Shop Area," September 11, 1923.

24. *Baltimore Sun*, "Max Hochschild Soon to Retire from Business: Will Retain Interest," June 2, 1927.

25. Alexander Gifford, "Max Hochschild Dies at 101," *Baltimore American*, June 2, 1957.

26. Gilbert Sandler, "Charge and Send," private essay.

27. Dick Wyman, interview with the author, March 5, 2012.

28. *Baltimore Sun*, "Department Store to Establish Branch at North Avenue and Charles Street," June 21, 1928.

29. Liz Moser, interview with the author, March 10, 2012.

30. Hochschild, Kohn & Co. archives, Maryland Historical Society.

31. *Baltimore Sun*, "Harundale Shopping Center Is Novel," September 7, 1958.

32. Gil Sandler, interview with the author.

33. *Evening Sun*, "Control of Hochschild, Kohn & Co. Sold to Western Investment Group," March 2, 1966.

34. Kohn, January 1979.

35. Ralph Simpson, "Columbia, Hochschild, Kohn Optimistic," *Baltimore Sun*, August 1, 1971.

36. Jesse Glasgow, "Security Hochschild, Kohn Store Opens Friday," *Baltimore Sun*, September 27, 1972.

37. Joseph J. Challmes, "Hochschild's in Edmondson Is to Close," *Baltimore Sun*, November 4, 1973.

38. Tracie Rozhon, "Plight of Downtown Stores: If Hochschild's Goes, Is Hutzler's Far Behind?" *Baltimore Sun*, January 23, 1977.

COME WHAT MAY

39. *Baltimore Sun*, Bernheimer-Leader Stores advertisement, May 1, 1925.

40. *Enterprising Emporiums*, 24.

41. *Baltimore News*, "May Company Buys Bernheimer-Leader Stores," September 9, 1927.

42. *Baltimore Sun*, "We Make Our Bow to Baltimore," May Company advertisement, September 10, 1927.

43. *Baltimore News-Post*, "Water Pipes Tampered With at May Co. Fire," February 25, 1947.

44. James Doran, interview with the author, March 20, 2012.

45. *Baltimore News-Post*, "Chief Cites Sabotage at Store Fire," February 25, 1947.

HECHT'S: THE HUB OF BALTIMORE

46. "The Hub: Golden Anniversary Year," company document, 1947.

47. *Baltimore Sun*, "Hecht's Will Mark Its 3rd Annual Founders Day," October 25, 1945.

48. Jacques Kelly, "The Hub of the Hecht Retailing Chain," *Baltimore News-American*, January 5, 1983.

49. *Baltimore Sun*, "Hecht Stores to Be Merged," October 4, 1951.

50. Bob Liston, "Hecht, May Firms Merger Boost to Downtown," *Baltimore American*, February 1, 1959.

51. Feinberg, *What Makes Shopping Centers Tick*, 65.

52. Jacquelyn R. Jackson, "Hecht, with Growing Competion, Is Wary but Hopeful," *Baltimore Sun*, May 27, 1983.

53. Feinberg, *What Makes Shopping Centers Tick*, 65.

54. *Evening Star*, "May Co. Will Consolidate D.C., Baltimore Hecht Units," February 22, 1973.

55. *Baltimore News-American*, "Hecht Co. Opens Store in Columbia Mall, Sees Record Year," August 3, 1975.
56. *Washington Post*, "Name Shift to Just Hecht's," April 26, 1978.

STEWART'S: ON THE WRONG SIDE OF THE STREET

57. *Enterprising Emporiums*, 27.
58. *Baltimore Sun*, "Posner Deal Closed," December 29, 1901.
59. *Baltimore Sun*, editorial, March 18, 1902.
60. Kenneth L. Miller, *Stewart's: A Louisville Landmark* (Louisville: Carraro Enterprises, 1991), 22.
61. *Baltimore Morning Herald*, "Negotiations to Close January 4," December 12, 1901.
62. Donald Alexander, interview with the author, February 21, 2012.
63. "A Brief 10-Year Review," Stewart & Co. document, 1938.
64. Will England, "City Stores 'King' Dies in Exile," *Baltimore Sun*, November 4, 1982.
65. Private conversation with former employee, spring 2011.
66. Jacques Kelly, interview with the author, March 21, 2012.

AND THE REST…

67. *Enterprising Emporiums*, 15.
68. Mary K. Zajac, "A Shopper's Emporium," *Style Magazine*, December 2011.
69. George C. Dorsch, "Store of Linens and Veteran Employes, O'Neill's Closes," *Baltimore Sun*, December 28, 1954.
70. Adele M. Hicks, "O'Neill's and Its Gentlemanly Owner," *Baltimore Sun*, December 2, 1979.
71. Zajac, "A Shopper's Emporium."
72. *Baltimore Sun*, "Thomas O'Neill Leaves Business to Employes," April 12, 1919.
73. Bob Eney, interview with the author, July 29, 2010.
74. J. Anthony Lukas, "Charles Center Demolition Starts," *Baltimore Sun*, January 6, 1961.

75. *Enterprising Emporiums*, 15.

76. *Baltimore Sun*, "Mrs. Gutman Mourned: Was One of Baltimore's Most Active Philanthropists," December 13, 1912.

77. Arthur Gutman, interview with the author, March 23, 2012.

78. Ibid.

79. Julius Westheimer, "Gutman's Known as the Popular Price Store," *Evening Sun*, December 27, 1984.

80. Henry Gutman, interview with the author, February 23, 2012.

81. *Baltimore Sun*, Woodward & Lothrop company advertisement, March 15, 1893.

82. Samuel Feinberg, "Capital Trading Areas," *Women's Wear Daily*, 1960.

83. Bobbie Gutman, interview with the author, February 23, 2012.

RUN RIGHT TO READ'S

84. Baltimore City Directory, 1899.

85. *Baltimore Sun*, "Shopping District Building Ready," September 1934.

86. Pinkney McLean, "Read Drug & Chemical to Mark 75th Year with Banquet," *Baltimore News-Post*, February 5, 1958.

87. Joe Nattans, interview with the author, June 10, 2012.

88. Ibid., February 10, 2012.

89. Alan Katz, interview with the author, July 23, 2010.

90. Carl Horn, interview with the author, July 22, 2010.

91. Kelly, interview.

SANTA CLAUS IS COMING TO TOWN

92. Jan Whitaker, *Service and Style: How the American Department Store Fashioned the Middle Class* (New York: St. Martin's Press, 2006), 119.

93. *Baltimore Magazine*, "Baltimore's Department Stores Present Attractive Pre-Christmas Show Windows," December 1941.

94. Ben Louis Posen, "I Remember…Staging the First Toytown Parade in Baltimore," *Baltimore Sun*, November 22, 1964.

95. William L. Bird, *Holidays on Display* (Princeton, NJ: Princeton Architectural Press, 2007), 69.

96. Bob Eney, interview with the author, January 31, 2012.

97. *Baltimore Sun*, "Store Cancels Toytown Parade," July 19, 1967.

WHITE SALE

98. Whitaker, *Service and Style*, 171.

99. *Enterprising Emporiums*, 38.

100. Ibid., 41.

101. *Baltimore Afro-American*, "Segragation Is Hurting Baltimore Department Store Business," March 8, 1930.

102. *Baltimore Afro-American*, "Report to What 'People'?" April 2, 1949.

103. Antero Pietila, Not in My Neighborhood (Chicago: Ivan R. Dee, 2010), 184.

104. *Baltimore Afro-American*, "Now Serve All," January 22, 1955.

105. *Baltimore Sun*, "Riots Start on Gay Street," April 7, 1968.

CLOSE OUT

106. Charleton Jones, "Is the Lexington Center Too Much, and Too Late?" *Baltimore Sun*, March 6, 1977.

107. Ted Shelby, "Hochschild Will Close Downtown Store in July, Sales Are Off, Subway Coming," *Baltimore Sun*, January 22, 1977.

108. *Baltimore Sun*, "Happy Chatter, Scribbled Notes, Welcome Chairs, and Gentle Pleasures," December 18, 1977.

109. Stacie Knable, "Hochschild's Is After What Others Aren't," *Evening Sun*, August 5, 1981.

110. James A. Rousmaniere Jr., "Stewart's May Close Downtown," *Baltimore Sun*, June 24, 1978.

111. *Baltimore News American*, "The Demise of Stewart's Downtown. Why?" January 3, 1979.

112. England, "City Stores 'King' Dies in Exile."

113. Rob Kasper, "Hutzler Memories: Shopping Tradition Lives On," *Baltimore Sun*, November 28, 1980.

114. Tracie Rozhon, "Store Officials List Downtown Woes," *Baltimore Sun*, July 14, 1978.

115. Hutzler Brothers Company board minutes, September 25, 1984.

116. Ellen Uzelac, "Hutzler's Hustles to Gain On Hecht," *Baltimore Sun*, November 25, 1984.

117. David Simon, "Brager Stores Closing Down; 180 Jobs Lost," *Baltimore Sun*, December 27, 1984.

118. Cindy Harper-Evans, "Epstein's, Victim of Slump, Closing All Stores," *Baltimore Sun*, January 19, 1991.

119. Joan Tyner, "Hutzler's Last Stand," *Maryland Business Weekly*, October 9, 1989.

120. Sherrie Clinton, "Hecht's Downtown Store to Close to Stop Red Ink," *Evening Sun*, October 19, 1988.

121. Joan Tyner, "Hecht's Store Closing Is 'End of an Era,'" *Baltimore Sun*, January 27, 1989.

122. Dan Thanh Dang, "Poor Hecht's: Losing its Place in the Retail World," *Baltimore Sun*, July 30, 2005.

123. Mary K. Zajac, "Final Sale," *Style Magazine*, May/June 2006.

Message Book

124. Private conversation with Governor William Donald Schaefer, July 2, 2009.

Tea for Two

125. Whitaker, *Service and Style*, 228–29.

126. John Dorsey, *Baltimore Sun* restaurant reviews, April 1, 1973; January 3, 1974; January 18, 1976; October 18, 1976.

About the Author

Michael J. Lisicky is the author of several bestselling books, including *Hutzler's: Where Baltimore Shops*. In demand as a department store historian, he has given lectures at institutions such as the New York Public Library, the Boston Public Library, the Free Library of Philadelphia, the Historical Society of Pennsylvania, the Carnegie Library of Pittsburgh, the Milwaukee County Historical Society, the Enoch Pratt Free Library and the Jewish Museum of Maryland. His books have received critical acclaim from the *Baltimore Sun, Baltimore City Paper, Philadelphia Inquirer, Philadelphia Daily News, Boston Globe, Boston Herald, Milwaukee Journal Sentinel* and *Pittsburgh Post Gazette*. He has been interviewed by national business periodicals including *Fortune Magazine, Investor's Business Daily* and *Bloomberg Businessweek*. His book *Gimbels Has It!* was recommended by National Public Radio's *Morning Edition* program as "One of the Freshest Reads of 2011." Mr. Lisicky helps run an "Ask the Expert" column with author Jan Whitaker at www.departmentstorehistory.net and resides in Baltimore, where he is an oboist with the Baltimore Symphony Orchestra.